Down the Kitchen Sink

Books by
Beverley Nichols

Down the Kitchen Sink

by

Beverley Nichols

Drawings by Val Biro

W. H. ALLEN · LONDON
A DIVISION OF HOWARD & WYNDHAM LTD
1974

For Avis Seed
The mistress of sans souci
with the author's love

PRINTED AND BOUND IN GREAT BRITAIN BY
BUTLER & TANNER LTD, FROME AND LONDON
FOR THE PUBLISHERS, W. H. ALLEN & CO. LTD
44 HILL STREET, LONDON WIX 8LB

ISBN 0 491 01551 8

Contents

PART ONE

CHAPTER I

Gaskin

IT was an evening in early spring and underneath the Eros statue the steps were piled high with the gold of primroses and the purple of violets, which the flower-girls were selling at tuppence a bunch. In and out of the traffic, like figures in a ballet, darted the newspaper boys, selling sheets which have long since fluttered into oblivion—the *Westminster Gazette*, which was printed on green paper and *The Globe* which was printed on pink; and *The Star*, whose pages needed no colour, for they sparkled and crackled with the brilliance of its prose. All at a penny apiece. There was a great deal of red in the picture, flashing from the uniforms of His Majesty's Life Guards, who carried themselves proudly, and seemed to be greatly enjoying themselves on their thirty shillings a week, as they joined up with their young ladies on the way to a two-shilling three-course dinner in Soho; where the waiters still said 'much obliged sir', and meant it, when they were presented with a shilling tip. And a great,

great deal of red in the sky, which glowed with the promise of a radiant tomorrow.

I strolled thoughtfully across Piccadilly Circus—(in those days, the early twenties, one could still wander about London like a gentleman, without courting the risk of instant death)—counting my blessings. They were many. I was twenty-five, and almost aggressively healthy. I was wearing a new suit in the latest fashion, with very wide trousers, which were flatteringly reflected in the plate glass windows. I was glowing with the fires of the latest thing in cocktails—the 'Sidecar'. I had consumed it in the long bar of the Trocadero—an enchanting grotto of delight, all gold mosaics and nouveau art, which should have been painted by Sickert, but never was. And only that morning I had corrected the proofs of my first entry in *Who's Who*. Not a very long entry, merely a couple of lines. But something inside me, probably the 'Sidecar', which was made of equal quantities of brandy, Cointreau and lemon juice, persuaded me that as the year went by, it would grow considerably longer. Which it did.

Yes, I should have been very happy, but I was not. For at home somebody was waiting for me whom I dreaded to meet.

The big clock over Fortnum and Mason's pointed to the hour of seven, and since I was not expected till seven-thirty it seemed a good idea to complete the rest of the journey on foot, in the hope of summoning up enough courage for the confrontation. This was not as simple as it sounds, for the wide pavements were thronged with ladies of the town, fluttering around like brightly coloured moths, dabbing at one's sleeve, whispering in one's ear, hastily cataloguing their accomplishments, usually in French, or rather in a Belgian argot, for we were still only a few years from the end of the First World War, with its flood of Belgian refugees. One of the salient differences between the contemporary London scene and the pageant of the twenties was provided by these ladies. They were instantly recognizable, by their large hats, their flaunting furs, their diamanté hand-bags, their aggressive perfumes—(we are still in the days of Chypre, 'jockey-club', and patchouli)—and their lavish employment of cosmetics. Today, in the seething chorus of Leicester Square, where every sexual fantasy has its appointed costume and maquillage, the appearance of such persons would suggest that they were on their way to a mother's meeting. But in the times of which I am writing, they were a race apart, with the authentic aura of wickedness. Whether they were more wicked than the scruffy crowds who throng the strip-club quarters of modern Soho is open to question; they were certainly more picturesque.

I quickened my footsteps, hurrying through the shadowy colonnade of the Ritz, crossing the road by the Berkeley, where the jeunesse dorée were beginning to drift into the grill-room, and so to Hyde Park Corner where I turned south towards Westminster. In the lemon-coloured twilight the still unravished façades of the city were a constant delight; no skyscrapers yet straddled the sky-line behind Buckingham Palace; the arrogant architectural obscenity of the Hilton hotel was mercifully hidden in the womb of time. And in the great squares, so strangely silent, the stately houses still bore the names of noble English families. No rash of brass plates had yet erupted in their porticos to announce their melancholy decline and conversion into flats—the soulless tenements of the rich.

My own house was far from great; indeed, it was one of the smallest in a little Victorian street that teetered about behind Harrods, rather apologetically, as though it felt that it had no right to trespass in the vicinity of so imposing an emporium. But it had a back-garden several sizes larger than a pocket-handkerchief, and it was adequate to provide accommodation for two of the essentials of civilized living—a grand piano and a cat.

And now I had acquired a third essential. A manservant. It was an awful thought, filling me with alarm and despondency, but the confrontation could no longer be avoided. I walked up the steps and turned the key.

He was waiting for me in the hall.

'Good evening, Gaskin.'

'Good evening, sir.'

He took my hat, as though to the manner born, and hung it up in the tiny cloakroom.

There was an awful silence. Had he been the French Ambassador or the Lord Chancellor, or a notorious criminal or anything simple like that, I should not have been at so total a loss. But he was a simple country lad, aged eighteen, whom I had engaged in a moment of madness, on the recommendation of my mother. She had discovered him in the depths of Norfolk, where one of my brothers had been suddenly rushed to a small country nursing-home after a serious accident. Apparently the whole of this primitive rustic establishment had revolved round the personality and energy of this young man; not only had he scrubbed the floors and made the beds, carried up the trays and washed the linen, but he had done the greater part of the cooking.

'He is an *excellent* cook,' my mother had said. 'And unless you are thinking of getting married . . .'

'I have no plans of that sort.'

'There's nobody you have not told me about?'

'Nobody.'

She sighed rather sadly. 'In that case, I think that you should snap him up. You work so hard. You have nobody but those dreadful daily women. You can't go on for ever living on snacks and sandwiches.'

'How much would he want?'

12

'I'm afraid it wouldn't be less than four pounds a week.'

It seemed a great deal of money, particularly as apart from paying his wages, I should also have to feed him. And indeed, in those days it *was* a great deal of money—about a fifth of my current income. To hell with it. I might write another book. I might get up earlier in the morning. When you are twenty-five, there is no end to the things you mightn't do. So I engaged him. And here he was standing before me, in a rather shabby suit, five feet ten inches of good Norfolk stock, pink-cheeked, bright-eyed, waiting for his instructions.

The awful silence persisted. I could think of nothing whatever to say. He had hung up my hat. I could hardly ask him to hang it up again. Nor did I feel inclined to begin a conversation about the weather. One did not employ manservants in order to discuss the weather. Or did one? I had no idea. In the whole complex of master–servant relationships I was as innocent as Gaskin himself. I was not yet a devotee of P. G. Wodehouse (who was later to become a dear and valued friend).

But Gaskin, though he was just as nervous as myself, had one great advantage over me. He was properly cast. He was a born Jeeves. He knew how to walk the stage, how to make his entrances and his exits, what lines to say and how to say them. He said the first one now.

'At what time,' he asked, 'will you be requiring dinner?'

Those, I swear, were his very words. They were delivered with a slight Norfolk accent, and with a hint of hesitation, as though he had pondered them, and learned them by heart. But those were his words. I was particularly touched by his use of the verb 'requiring'.

The ice was broken. I said . . .

'Shall we say eight o'clock?'

'Certainly, sir.'

'Downstairs?'

'Of course, sir.'

The dialogue was getting quite sparkling.

'Have you . . . er . . . got anything in particular?' (Not a brilliant line, but it served its purpose.)

'I thought . . . a nice little sole, sir.'

Better and better. A nice little sole was just what the doctor ordered. Even had it been a nasty little sole I could have coped with it.

'Did you get it at Harrods? I have an account there.'

'No, sir. I went to Harrods. But I was not impressed.'

This was enchanting. Gaskin—peasant stock, shabbily suited—Gaskin, who had never been on a bus nor travelled in a tube—Gaskin, who had not yet blinked at the bright lights of Piccadilly—was not impressed by Harrods.

'So where did you get it?'

'There is a fish shop at the end of the street, sir. The lady who owns it made me a special price. She comes from Norfolk.'

Later, as our association developed, I was to learn that an astonishing number of the tradesmen with whom we came to deal seemed to come from Norfolk. They were like a vast secret society.

'That will be nice for you, to have a friend nearby.'

He inclined his head, but with no great enthusiasm. I suspected that he had higher ambitions than ladies in fish shops.

There seemed nothing more to say for the moment, so I went upstairs to my bedroom whose windows were shadowed by the branches of an ancient laburnum that still had enough life in it to pay a few golden dividends. On the patchwork quilt he had laid out my dinner clothes. The links were in the dress-shirt, with the black tie neatly folded across the collar. The shoes were newly burnished, and a fresh linen handkerchief sprouted from the breast pocket of the dinner-jacket. Feeling slightly intimidated I repaired to the bathroom, where I was greeted with further evidence of his activities. My dressing-gown had been washed and ironed, and the towels, instead of cluttering the floor, were arranged on the towel rack with immaculate precision.

But the most startling and unexpected example of his efforts awaited me on the ledge over the wash-basin. I stared at it with dismay. It was a glass filled with luke-warm water, and across it he had laid my tooth-brush, onto which he had squeezed the requisite amount of pink tooth-paste, so daintily disposed that it recalled the icing on a Christmas cake.

'This,' I said to myself with mounting alarm, 'has got to stop. C'est magnifique, mais ce n'est pas moi. If Gaskin thinks that I am going to come home after a sweaty day in Fleet Street, dress for dinner, and languidly stretch out my hand in order to anoint my gleaming ivories with pre-conditioned tooth-paste, he has something coming to him.' However, it would have been cruel to disillusion him on this first night. So I had my bath, dressed, and went down to dinner.

He was standing behind my chair in the tiny dining-room. He had a napkin over his arm, and he looked strangely excited, as though he were a lad embarking on a great adventure, serving a master who was sailing into perilous seas. In both of these similes he would not have been so far from the truth.

It was a very simple dinner, and I shall never forget it, though I could not give a list of the little plate of cheap but imaginative hors d'œuvres with which it began. But the main course . . . that was what proclaimed his genius, and it established a standard which he was to sustain for nearly forty years. It was a Sole Colbert, at the peak of perfection—delicate in the centre, exquisitely crisp outside, cradling its content of savoury butter, at precisely the right temperature, and flavoured with a mixture of freshly chopped parsley and mixed herbs.

I finished it to the last morsel and called through the doorway.

'Thank you, Gaskin. That was delicious.'

'Will that be all, sir?'

'I think so.'

'Will you be taking coffee, sir?'

'If it isn't too much trouble.'

A fleeting expression of reproach informed me that this remark was not well received. The perfect Jeeves does not expect his master to consider whether things are too much trouble. I must remember this in future.

There is not much more to record about this first night. After he had cleared away the coffee things he reappeared, and asked if he might go out for a walk. I said of course. And when he enquired what time I wished him to be in, I informed him that it was a matter of indifference to me, as long as he got back in time to give me breakfast. This remark *was* well received. It was evidently in the right Jeeves tradition.

I have no idea when he got back. I slept too well, in pyjamas that had been freshly ironed, and a bed that had been properly made, solaced by the memory of the perfect Sole Colbert.

CHAPTER 2

The Making of a Manservant

THIS is supposed to be a cookery book, but I suspect that it will turn out to be something rather different. True, it will contain a number of Gaskin's own recipes, which, after his death, I found interlarded among the pages of the cookery books that he had collected over the years. These were sometimes scribbled over with mysterious comments on the guests who were likely to partake of them, such as 'No crab for Lady F'. I cannot remember any Lady F in my life, nor why she should have been denied this delicacy. It will also contain accounts of various epicurean occasions which, for one reason or another, have lingered in my memory. Finally, it will record my own struggles when, late in life, I suddenly found myself left alone, standing in a deserted kitchen, staring at a stove which I had never learned to light, surrounded by pots and pans of whose functions I was totally ignorant, and wondering, with a heavy heart, what I was going to do about it. The idea of getting 'another Gaskin' was unthinkable. There never could be another Gaskin, either for myself or probably for anybody else. The race is extinct and can never be recreated. For this reason, if for no other, Gaskin deserves his little niche in social history.

On the following morning, at eight o'clock precisely, there was a knock on the door, and he appeared with my breakfast tray. Coffee, eggs and bacon, toast, freshly rolled butter, marmalade, and *The Times*, the *Daily Telegraph* and the *Daily Express* tucked under his arm. He drew the curtains, letting in the sunlight, which shone on the few brave golden tassels which were still being produced by the indomitable old laburnum.

This, I thought, stretching myself, is the life. And—speaking of life, with the benefit of hindsight—I may mention that this breakfast routine, in the years to come, was to be repeated some fourteen thousand times. It sounds like something from the old strip cartoon 'Believe it or not'. Fourteen thousand breakfasts in bed? Surely not? In these days, when a millionairess considers herself lucky if she can bribe a heavily moustached Portuguese au pair girl to give her breakfast in bed for six consecutive weeks, it sounds too good to be true. But it is true. He was with me for nearly forty years, he always gave me breakfast in bed, and if we multiply forty by 365 we arrive at the figure of 14,600, unless our arithmetic is at fault.

The morning was brilliantly sunny, and when I had shaved and brushed my teeth with the predecorated tooth-brush, I called downstairs and told him to get ready for a visit to the tailors. This was a responsibility that I had undertaken before engaging him, and an urgent one, for though he was spick and span, and bright as a new pin, his suit was shiny and I guessed that it was the only one he had.

I went out to fetch the car, which was housed in a scruffy garage round the corner. Life, I reflected, was quickening, not only for me, but for many young men of that period who were my friends, and still are. Only a few days before, Noël Coward had seized me by the arm, announcing, of all things, that he had just acquired a *secretary*. He was so excited that it sounded as though he had invested in a mistress. And it was indeed front page news, which made me feel rather jealous. Never mind. I had acquired a manservant, and in the scale of eternal values a manservant must surely rank as high as a secretary, if not higher. And I was going to take him to the tailors in my very own car. It was a small two-seater Renault, which I had bought because it was the colour of forget-me-nots.

If I had paused for a moment, in this headlong rush towards these rarified heights, I might not have been so complacent. The tailors whom we were visiting would have to give me credit. As for the car, I had purchased it on a three year plan, and there were still thirty-five monthly instalments to be met. The rent was due at the end of the month, and Harrods' last bill had a rather sinister slip attached to it, in red ink. But I did not pause. For I was sustained by one tangible asset—a book called *Twenty-Five*—which had just been published and, so I assured myself, would become a best-seller. As it happened, it did, though I was not to know this at the time.

He was waiting for me on the doorstep, hat in hand. In the bright sunlight his suit was shinier than ever, his tie was frayed, and his hat had obviously seen better days. Were it not for a certain innate dignity in his bearing, a curious assurance, he might have been a country yokel, up for the day. But there was nothing bucolic about his comments on the passing scene.

We drove up Sloane Street, into Knightsbridge, and skirted the park, where the tulips were coming into blossom.

'This,' I told him, 'is Hyde Park Corner.'

'Yes, sir, I came here last night.'

'Did you have a good time?'

'I kept myself to myself, sir.'

This was said with a faint echo of reproach. My question, evidently, was not the sort which should have been addressed to the perfect Jeeves.

We were held up in a traffic jam. He looked straight ahead.

'Would that be Piccadilly, sir?'

'Yes. Do you want to go down it?'

'If it is not taking you out of your way, sir.'

As we neared the Ritz I sensed that he was beginning to get excited. 'Is there anything you'd particularly care to see?'

He hesitated for a moment. Then, nervously twirling his hat—(he was the country boy again)—he said, 'I believe Mr Hugh Walpole lives in these parts.'

This was such a totally unexpected observation that I almost ran into a bus.

'Yes, he does. In fact, we're just passing his flat. Why do you ask?'

'He is one of my favourite authors, sir. Are you acquainted with him?'

'Yes, I am.'

This revelation of Gaskin's literary taste was somewhat embarrassing, because I had written some rather caustic comments about Hugh Walpole in *Twenty-Five*, which had not been at all well received. I hoped that Gaskin would not expect me to ask him to dinner. As things turned out, he did come to dinner on more than one occasion in the years ahead, and whatever hard feelings he may have entertained were forgotten when Gaskin led him into his sitting-room, and showed him a complete set of his own works, so worn and tattered with constant reading that some of them were almost illegible.

We turned up Bond Street, and now his eyes began to

pop. By a happy chance, a number of celebrities were taking the air and, though I might not know them personally, I was able to identify them for him. Here, for example, was the Earl of Lonsdale, sitting outside Cartiers, glowering at the passers-by from his eccentric barouche, which was the colour of dandelions and was known as the Yellow Peril. As we drove past him, I took off my hat and waved it at him—a gesture which had a marked effect on Gaskin and an even more marked effect on the Earl, because we had never met. Here, too, was Gladys Cooper, looking incredibly beautiful, stepping out of Asprey's. Another wave, which this time was returned. As we entered Grosvenor Square, I turned to the right, so that I could regale him with a sight of the house of the celebrated Lady Cunard, which was Number 4, at the corner of Brook Street. A very beautiful black poodle was sitting on the steps, sunning itself. I waved at this too, and I should have waved even more vigorously if I had known that before long it was to become the father of a dog of my very own. For one day the poodle got bored with his ladyship, and crossed the Square to call at the Chinese Embassy, which was the residence of a very alluring black chow. Romance was born, and Emerald Cunard gave me one of the results—a black poodle, with a chow tail and a black spot on the tip of its tongue.

And now at last we arrived at the tailor's shop, which proved to be a small, genteel, rather shabby, and extremely Dickensian establishment at the corner of Duke Street. It dealt exclusively in suits for gentlemen's gentlemen, and it had been recommended to me by Michael Arlen, which was as it should be. For he too, under the guise of fiction, was much concerned with gentlemen, and eventually, after a great deal of hard work, managed to become one himself, or something very like it.

But the word 'gentleman' disturbed me. I could not

hear myself going into the shop and saying, 'This is my gentleman's gentleman. Please fit him for a pair of trousers.' That would have sounded more than somewhat odd. Nor could I see myself hovering about while they put tape measures round his waist. I was pretty sure that his undergarments were patchy, so, partly through cowardice and partly, I hope, through consideration, I gave him my card and told him to get on with it.

When I picked him up again, he was standing on the door step, with a beaming smile. The ordeal had evidently been triumphantly surmounted.

'Did they fix you up all right?'

'Yes, sir, thank you very much.'

'What did you get?'

'A single-breasted poplin, sir. Dark grey. And a double-breasted pin-stripe. Dark blue. For more formal occasions.'

'I thought you were going to get three suits? What about the short white jacket?'

'I did not think, sir, that it would be quite the Thing.'

Touché again. The unerring instinct of the perfect Jeeves had put me in my place. I had rather hankered for the short white jacket, hovering in the background. I had even dreamed of a striped maroon waistcoat and a green apron, after the style of a valet in a French château. If Noël Coward had ever brought his secretary to luncheon, I should certainly have required Gaskin to wear these things, though not, perhaps, all at once. However, Gaskin had decided that they would not be quite the 'Thing'.

The Thing. What was it? Who told him about it? Was it evidence of innate breeding, inherited from some distant ancestor? The good old Norfolk name of Gaskin, obviously, derived from the French Gascoigne, which has echoes of nobility. The Thing?

Perhaps it was simply a matter of natural good taste. There was certainly nothing wrong with the taste of my luncheon, which he served on our return from this youthful, spring-time excursion. In the old days I should have munched a sandwich, or gone over to the pub for a bitter and a sausage roll. As it was, I sat down to a soufflé, à point, served in a very pretty pale blue dish which he had discovered in the coal-shed. He had encircled it in a white napkin, and as I consumed it I recalled the immortal remark of Oscar Wilde, who expressed his determination to 'live up to his blue china'.

Evidently the future demanded that I should live up to Gaskin, and the rest of this book will record how I endeavoured to do so.

So began the era of Reginald Arthur Gaskin—gentleman's gentleman—the last, and maybe among the most distinguished, of the great Jeeves' fraternity. If I had known that it was to endure for a life-time, I would have noted it in finer detail, plotted it and charted it, recorded it in diaries and painted it on canvases more lasting than the tablets of memory. He certainly deserved such a tribute. Even so, the memories are vivid enough.

The memory, for example, of my first Bright Young People party, which was in honour of Tallulah Bankhead. This, I had fondly imagined, was just the sort of party that Gaskin would enjoy. He had swiftly disclosed himself as an ardent theatre-goer, spending most of his small salary on gallery seats for West End productions. His favourite was *The Maid of the Mountains*, and he had a photograph of Jose Collins pinned up over his bed. When he heard that I had composed a waltz song for her, entitled *Too Soon*, he was greatly impressed, and asked if we might listen to it together, when it was broadcast, which we did, or rather, which we should have done if it had ever been broadcast. But alas, on this occasion, Jose was 'not herself'. She was an enchanting singer, and a fine actress, and altogether a very charming person, but she was not always abstemious. She mislaid the score in a taxi, and instead of my little waltz, which was quite pretty, all we got was the voice of the compère announcing that Mr Beverley Nichols' new ballad, entitled *Too Soon*, had unfortunately arrived too late.

Tallulah, I fondly imagined, would have an even greater attraction for Gaskin than Jose. She was the toast of the town, starring in *The Dancers* with Gerald du Maurier—radiantly beautiful, and apparently quite exceptionally immoral. Anybody, one was assured, could go to bed with Tallulah, regardless of gender, shape, size, or social position. I believe that it was Tallulah whom Noël Coward had in mind when he wrote of the young lady who 'used sex like a shrimping net'.

So the party should have been a great success, and as far as Gaskin's part in it was concerned, it was. The buffet was a triumph piece, with cold lobster soup, several varieties of mousse, exquisitely decorated, home-made meringues in which the cream had been delicately tinged with crème de menthe, and for a hot course, the best kedgeree I had ever tasted. All out of his own head.

But his master-stroke was the red carpet. When he first suggested that we should have one I was not enthusiastic. I thought a red carpet would be rather pretentious.

'I was passing through Grosvenor Square the other night, sir, and I observed that there were several red carpets outside the great houses.'

'But this is not Grosvenor Square, and we aren't expecting royalty.'

'No, sir. What's more, it might rain.'

'But where should we *get* a red carpet?'

'There are Establishments, sir, which deal with such things.'

'Do you know any . . . er . . . Establishments?'

'I have made enquiries, sir.'

In the face of such persistence there was nothing to be done but to let him have his carpet. Alas, it was to prove our undoing. For in the small hours of the morning, when the party was breaking up, Tallulah decided that she would like to go for a ride on it. This seemed a splendid idea, and several of us—one of them I believe was Patrick Balfour, who today, under the name of Lord Kinross, is a distinguished historian—tumbled outside, spread the carpet in the middle of the street, and deposited Tallulah on it, making so much noise, as we did so, that lights began to be switched on in neighbouring houses, and windows were flung open, revealing scandalized faces. Where did she wish to go, we enquired? The House of Commons, she informed us, in somewhat blurred accents. To be presented to the Speaker. Of course. The obvious place and the obvious person. He would be enchanted. So off we charged, to the strains of the Eton Boating Song. The night was balmy, the moon was high, the surface of the road was dry and highly polished, the streets were deserted, and we made excellent progress until we came into the arms of the law. Quite literally into the arms of the law. The last I remember of that night was the vision of Tallulah, hair flying, sequins glittering in the moonlight, throwing her arms round the neck of a handsome young constable, and informing him, in the throaty accents of Alabama, that British policemen were wonderful.

Re-enter Jeeves. When Gaskin woke me up on the following morning—or rather, three hours later—he did not draw the curtains. Subdued lights, he had rightly opined, would be more appropriate to this occasion. And when he placed the breakfast tray on the side-table there were no eggs and bacon. Only a large glass, misted on the outside, proclaiming its chilliness, filled with a murky mixture which I recognized as a Prairie Oyster. Two raw eggs, a tablespoonful of Worcester sauce, and a teaspoonful of liqueur brandy.

I struggled up onto the pillows, clutched the glass, and swallowed. There is a certain technique to be observed in swallowing Prairie Oysters, which even to this day I have not fully mastered, maybe because there have not been so many occasions when I have needed them. One must open the mouth very wide, close the eyes, take a deep breath, and gulp, trying as one does so to keep the mind on Higher Things, which is not really so very difficult, because there are a great many Higher Things than swallowing two raw eggs in a glutinous mixture of brandy and Worcester sauce.

'Thank you. That was just what I needed.'

'Quite, sir.'

Silence. Something, evidently, was amiss, and I had a shrewd suspicion what it was. Gaskin was feeling that he had been 'put upon', and he was quite right. He had been cooking for two days, serving drinks and food for six hours, and I hated to think how long he must have spent washing up, sweeping carpets, clearing away broken glasses. Still, I had to say something.

'I thought the party was a great success. Everybody loved the kedgeree.'

'Thank you, sir.'

'Miss Bankhead had three helpings.'

He opened his mouth, and closed it again. He was keeping himself to himself.

He took my glass, placed it gently on the tray, and went to the door. There he turned.

In icy tones, he observed, 'I believe, sir, that Miss Bankhead was *born* a lady.'

Exit.

But in spite of this veneer of sophistication, the almost uncanny facility with which he was stepping into the role of Jeeves—of whom he had probably never heard—he was still the country boy at heart. He was still rather frightened of London; he may even have been rather frightened of myself. And he was lonely.

A few days after the party he came up to me as I was

getting ready to set out for Fleet Street. 'Excuse me, sir, may I mention something? I read an article about you in a Ladies' Magazine, which said that you were very partial to cats.'

'I am, very partial.'

'Well, sir, the lady in the fish shop has a kitten, and she was wondering . . .'

A long pause. I had no doubt what the lady in the fish shop was wondering, but the acquisition of a kitten is such a tremendous step in life that it had to be given a certain amount of thought.

'Do you think we are quite ready for a kitten?'

'I would look after it, sir. It would be no trouble at all. And if she can't find a home for it she will have to have it put away.'

The pleading in his eyes was difficult to resist. Even so . . .

'It isn't a female, is it?'

'Oh no, sir . . . not at all. Black, it is, with white paws. And a very loud purr.'

This was sheer blackmail. Black with white paws. And a very loud purr. Gaskin knew that he had won.

'In that case, sir,' he said—and he seemed to be purring, ever so faintly, himself—'I will see to the BOX.'

As it happened, he had already done so. For as I went to fetch my hat from the little cloakroom I noticed, in the corner, a wooden box standing on a piece of newspaper, and by its side, a bag of sand.

I had a busy day, the sort of day which may serve as a contrast to the rather jeunesse dorée existence which I seem to have been describing. A typical Fleet Street reporter's day. It began with a visit to the Zoo, to write a story about a temperamental elephant which had suddenly gone on strike and refused to carry any more children on its back, at sixpence a time. After taking a good look at the children I had every sympathy with the elephant. The day continued with a visit to a woman who

27

had given birth to a six-toed baby. A difficult assignment, this, which demanded a subtle and rather revolting blend of whimsicality and pathos. ('Say anything you like when writing about babies' my editor had warned me, 'but never treat them as a joke.' I never did.) During the afternoon there was a great deal of telephoning from the office, asking various celebrities their opinion of this, that and the other. Before dinner I had to scurry round the House of Commons in search of a Labour MP who had reputedly said something offensive about the Royal Family, and after dinner—a Welsh rarebit at the Falstaff in Fleet—I had to sit in the overheated dressing-room of a musical comedy star in order to ascertain her views on life after death. She had none, but I made some up for her, with marked effect. As a result of the story which I wrote about her she gained a reputation for psychic erudition which was almost fatal to her career.

All this at three guineas a column for 'news' pages, and four guineas a column for 'feature' pages. And all, as I suggested before, in vivid contrast with the picture of the gilded young gentleman being waited upon, hand and foot, by his gentleman's gentleman. What it really meant, of course, was that I was leading two lives, and maybe making a failure of both of them. But at least I was living.

Midnight, and back to the little house, dead tired, but nearly ten pounds to the good. Back to quietness, and to comfort, away from the roar of Fleet Street. Back to Gaskin, the symbol of the other sort of life, for which I was striving. And back—I suddenly remembered—to a kitten.

I tiptoed into the hall, treading very softly, for it might be asleep, and sleeping kittens, particularly when they are new arrivals, should not be disturbed. But where? On the sofa—under the piano—in a fold of the curtains? Then, looking upstairs, I guessed where it would be. I had a sharp but painful twinge of jealousy. It would be with Gaskin. Black coat, white paws, loud purr, and all.

Up the stairs. My fingers on the handle of his bed-room door. Turn it very gently. Since he always slept with the windows open, and the curtains drawn back, there was enough light in the room to see that he was not alone. Nestling under his shoulder was a small furry object, the size of a teacup. A black teacup. As I stayed there the teacup moved, stretched out a languid paw, and opened one green eye. Opened it, and closed it again. 'J'y suis,' the teacup seemed to be saying. 'J'y reste.' I closed the door again, and went to bed.

If Gaskin had disliked cats I doubt whether he would have lasted for a couple of months. Sooner or later there would have been a crisis, a battle of wills, and the cat, of course, would have won, ably assisted by myself. All the breakfasts-in-bed, all the soufflés, all the elegant mystique with which he had invested my life would have had to be sacrificed. In the twenties there was a popular parlour game called 'Two on the Tower'—a sort of variation of the Truth Game. In this game you had to imagine that you were on the top of a tall tower with a friend on either side, or maybe an enemy, and you had to confess to the assembled company which of them you would push off first. These games were played with passionate intensity, and more than once led to tragedy. I hope that it will not lead to tragedy if I confess that if I were in such a situation, with a cat on one side and a certain type of man on the other, the man would be the first to go. Our arrogant assumption that the life of a human being is of greater importance than the life of an animal is a major cause of our current distraction and distress.

CHAPTER 3

April in Paris

SINCE this is supposed to be a cookery book, we will turn the clock forwards, for the space of one year, and switch the scene to Paris.

The milieu is grand, indeed glittering. We are seated at a long dining table in one of the city's most beautiful houses . . . Number 25 Rue de Surène, the Norwegian Embassy, where we are staying. There are so many appurtenances of luxury that an Edwardian novelist would have been in his element. The women are 'superbly gowned'—the silver has 'a diamond sparkle'—we are drinking the 'choicest wines'—and, needless to say, we are being served by 'silent footmen'. (With the exception of one poor young man who has some sort of bother with his stomach, and rumbles like a rattle-snake when he bends over to serve the lobster mousse.)

Dinner is drawing to a close. Conversation is flagging, because our host is getting rather bored by the lady on his right. Then the double doors swing open; there is a flash of silver trays and a flutter of Meissen plates; and before each of us, served by the white-gloved hands of the aforesaid silent footman, appears a culinary poem. A delicate silver bubble, crowned with a jade-green leaf of rose-geranium.

Whereupon my heart leapt up as though I had beheld a rainbow in the sky. For I recognized the rose-geranium, which had been picked from my own back garden. And I realized who had created the culinary poem. Gaskin. The country lad whom I had brought with me to Paris.

That was the sort of cook he was. He thought ahead. He had naturally been very excited when I told him that he was coming with me to Paris, but though he walked on air he did not lose his head. He decided, entirely on his own initiative, that he would show the cook what *he* could do. He was not to know that there were two cooks, both masters, working in a kitchen as big as a house. But even if he had known he would not have been dismayed. He would still have insisted on making his syllabub from the old country recipe which he had learnt in his Norfolk village. When he had first made it for me, I asked him why he had decorated it with a leaf of rose-geranium. 'Because they go together, sir,' he said. If you pinch a leaf between your fingers when you are eating this delicious concoction, you will see what he meant.

Here is the recipe.

Syllabub (for four people)
In case you are entertaining any scholars to dinner it might be helpful to know that the Oxford Dictionary definition of Syllabub dates the word from 1537 and describes its origin as 'obscure'. The dictionary will not be much help in concocting it, dismissing it as 'a drink or dish made of milk or cream, curdled by the admixture of wine or acid'. However, there is the additional information that by the year 1706 the word had acquired a symbolic meaning, to indicate 'anything unsubstantial or frothy; e.g. floridly vapid discourse or writing'. This

might come in handy, particularly when discussing fellow authors.

There are numerous recipes, most of them cumbersome and fussy. Mrs Beeton's is definitely to be avoided, for she insists upon the inclusion of macaroons, which have no historical gastronomic connection. To make matters worse, she adds something called 'Ratafia essence'. If you were to ask for this at the average grocers you would be met with a steely glare and asked to move-along please. My own recipe, compiled from Gaskin's notes, is simple, and though luxurious, not terribly expensive.

But it *must* be started two days before it is eaten. To make this crystal clear, we will use days.

Monday. Take 2 lemons, peel with a sharp knife, squeeze juice into a bowl, add rinds and one large wine glass of brandy. Leave in larder.

Tuesday. Pour ¼ lb of caster sugar into the bowl, adding a sprinkling of ground cinnamon. Stir until dissolved. Into a separate bowl pour ½ pint of double cream and whip with a balloon whisk until it is just beginning to stand up. Crisis moment. Still whipping like mad, add the contents of the first bowl, *very* gradually, or the whole thing will turn into a mass of ectoplasm, only suitable to be served at supper-parties for retired spiritualists.

Pour into glasses, and dab into shape with dainty finger tips. (This 'finger tip dabbing' almost calls for a chapter in itself. I am quite sure that most cooks, in emergencies, do a lot of manual manipulations in the kitchen which they would hate their guests to know about.)

Wednesday. Take out of refrigerator and devour.

Postscript on Decorations. Gaskin's syllabub, as we have noted, was adorned with a leaf of rose-geranium. The one thing with which you must not adorn it is a bottled cherry. Bottled cherries are the quintessence of nastiness in whatever form they are served, tasting of mouth-wash, and recalling the lipsticks of undesirable barmaids.

The episode of the syllabub established Gaskin firmly in the affection of our host, the Ambassador, whom we might now pause to consider because the way of life that he had created for himself is seldom encountered in the modern world. His name was Baron Frederick Wedel-Jarlsberg. The Wedel family, in one form or another, have been prominent in the history of Scandinavia ever since it had any history at all. They seem to have castles scattered all over North-Western Europe. Baron Frederick showed his quality at a very early age; he was only twenty-eight when he came to England, made friends with King Edward the Seventh, and personally negotiated a vital treaty between Norway and Sweden whose main outlines have endured to this day. After which, he fell in love with a girl who happened to be very rich, and married her. When she died he fell in love with another girl who happened to be even richer, and married her. The love, in each case and on both sides, was genuine and lasting, whatever the cynics may say.

The Baron was about seventy, tall, commanding, resonant of voice. His eyes were as bright as a young man's and his pink cheeks were unwrinkled. He used to slap them every morning with a special sort of eau de cologne that he bought in the Haymarket. Not that *he* bought it; his English valet, whose name was Alfred, was sent over to London to buy it.

One day I suggested that it might be simple if it were sent by post.

'No,' he replied. 'It is better that Alfred buys it.'

'But why?'

'Because Alfred has a chère amie in London. She is very fot . . .' (he meant 'fat', but he could not pronounce the short English 'a'.) 'And he luffs her. She is fot like the devil, but he luffs her. And if he did not see her, he would leave me.'

The Baron gave me a taste for luxury which might have been demoralizing, and nearly was. For example, when we went to the opera we drove up in an immense Isotta-Fraschini, encased in chinchilla rugs which had been deftly arranged over our knees by a young man who lived in the concierge's lodge, and appeared to have no other occupation but rug-arranging. On our arrival, the traffic miraculously melted away, and we slid out of our rugs and walked across a pavement from which the public seemed to be momentarily excluded. They must have thought that we were some sort of royalty. We always had the royal box—or whatever the equivalent of the royal box may be in Paris. And when we returned to the Embassy, the lights in the entire house suddenly blazed as soon as we swept into the great courtyard, the doors swung open, and there under the chandelier stood the butler and at least two footmen, plus, of course, the young rug-removing gentleman. Whereupon, we slowly ascended the vast staircase, said goodnight to the Baroness, and repaired to one of several Louis Seize salons to discuss the evening's entertainment over a bottle of iced Vichy water and a silver platter of Bath Oliver biscuits.

The Baron's comments were given an extra poignancy by the fact that though he spoke English with great fluency, his accent had so marked a Scandinavian timbre that sometimes one was puzzled. Thus, on one occasion when he was slapping his cheeks with the aforesaid eau de cologne, he winced and said something which sounded even more Scandinavian than usual.

I enquired if anything was the matter.

'I have a pain in my tum,' he barked.

After last night's dinner, I reflected, this was hardly surprising. 'Can I get you anything for it? A little chlorodyne?'

He flashed a look of scorn and held out his hand. It was his thumb, not his stomach, that was affected.

He was quite incapable of pronouncing 'th'. We had not been to the theatre, we had been to the 'teatre', where the leading lady had given a 'trilling' performance. If he were an impresario he would back her through 'tick and tin'. Nor could he pronounce the short 'u'. He could not wish you good luck; it became good 'lok'. A bad play was 'mok'. And so it was with all combinations in which the sound of 'uck' was called for.

And now, for the first and almost certainly the last time in a long career, I find myself constrained to tell a story containing a four-letter word. It is a very slight story, of which the only point is the four-letter word itself, but it has sometimes made me smile when I have remembered it over the years.

It happened in the small hours of the morning, when I returned to the Rue de Surène after a night on the town. As may be imagined, there were many dinner parties in the Embassy which would have bored me, and from these I was mercifully excluded.

No 'Je ne veux pas que tu t'ennuie, mon cher,' the Baron would say. 'There are four women who come, and they are all fot like the devil. One of them, she has une grosse fortune, but she has also une grosse moustache. Tu es trop jeune et trop beau pour une telle vache . . . attends un petit instant.' Whereupon he would produce his wallet and extract a thousand franc note, which in those days was the equivalent of at least fifty dollars.

All he required in exchange for this largesse was a smile, and a brief resumé of my experiences when I came home.

My first port of call on these expeditions was a café in the Rue Royale, where I went in order to change the Baron's note into smaller denominations. One never knew where one would land up before the night was out.

Having changed the notes I would carefully conceal them in various parts of my clothing where they would not be too easily available to any disreputable characters with whom one might strike up an acquaintance. For the information of those who have led comparatively sheltered lives this procedure is not as simple as it sounds. The most difficult part is stuffing fifty franc notes into one's socks. One has to hoist up the right leg with the left hand —glancing over the shoulder to ensure that one is not observed—and then, after a fortifying glass of pernod, slide the notes over the ankle and, if possible, under the heel. About two hundred francs were usually disposed of in this manner, the other notes being pinned under the lapels of my jacket or artfully folded in the handkerchief-pocket. It was a charming prelude to dinner, and the only drawback was that for the rest of the evening one was inclined to produce rustling noises from unexpected places as though one were a sort of perambulating waste-paper basket.

And then . . . Paris by night! Young, agile, more than somewhat romantic, wildly experimental, and for the moment as rich as Croesus. I usually began in the Rue de Lappe, which was a street of exquisite squalor, throbbing to the music of concertinas, and thronged with the figures of dancing sailors. In those days the Rue de Lappe had not yet become a tourist attraction, it was all 'le vrai', and pleasurably precarious, for sometimes there were knives in the sailors' pockets and the fingers of their girl friends were very nimble. The only 'respectable' person one ever saw there—though the adjective is perhaps inapposite—was Jean Cocteau, sitting in a corner, drawing sketches on the top of a marble table. I liked Cocteau, and he was wildly funny on occasions, but he gave me the creeps because he smelt of opium. And however irregular my conduct I never had any desire to experiment in drugs.

My romances in the Rue de Lappe and similarly

dubious thoroughfares have no place in a cookery book. All that need concern us is the return to the Rue de Surène. Rather fuzzy but reasonably intact. Most of the money gone. Dear Baron. It is all thanks to him. He will be waiting up for me—eager for the story of my adventures. The only trouble is that there usually *are* no adventures. Admittedly, one has mixed in strange company and danced to stranger music, but there it has usually ended. I suppose that the main thrill was the sense of danger—what Wilde meant when he spoke of 'supping with panthers'. But it would never do to admit this to the Baron. He was a dear old gentleman, in whom the fires still flickered, and he wanted his story, he pined for the vicarious pleasure of my youthful ardours.

Very well, he should have his story. I think I learned more about the technique of writing fiction, during those slow and rather tottery ascents of the great staircase in the Embassy, than I should have learned in years of professional practice. For as I sat opposite him, gratefully imbibing the iced Vichy water, my imagination took wings. I had done this, that, and the other, and often both at once. I had achieved feats of amorous endurance which would have knocked Don Juan for six. Anything any young man in Paris could do, I could and had done, and a great deal better.

Were my stories getting home? They were. A glow of gentle appeasement illuminated the Baron's face. I was paying my debt. And was that all? Yes, I would think, it was, for his eyelids were beginning to droop, and my own potencies, fictional and physical, were about exhausted.

Whereupon—here at last is the beginning, the middle, and the end of our story—he rises to his feet, pats me on the shoulder, and murmurs, in tones of avuncular approval, a phrase which in the terms of my own small life has a claim to immortality.

'You tink of notting but fok.'

It was not true. I thought of a great many other things than fok. The lights on the Seine, the scented corridors of the Ritz, the dark staircase of the maison de rendezvous in the Passage Saumon, the splintered kaleidoscope of coloured glass seen through the window of a taxi as one swept up the hill to the Place Pigalle, in the small hours of the morning. None of these things had anything to do with fok, though I suppose that it lurked in the mental and physical background.

But I never contradicted the Baron; it would have spoiled his pleasure in the lovely evening which he had given me, for which I thank him over the years.

I also thank him for unwittingly giving me the opportunity to prove that I am a thoroughly contemporary writer, who can use a four-letter word as aptly as any of my juniors, even if it becomes a three-letter word in the process.

RECIPES

Melon Jarlsberg

While we were in Paris Gaskin did not waste the time he spent in the Baron's kitchens, and collected a number of recipes from the head chef. Most of them were beyond my means; they seemed to demand crates of lobsters and tureens of caviar. But there were a few that were exotic without being exorbitant, and among them was the Jarlsberg Melon.

You eat this melon, ideally, with Parma ham, though it is almost as delicious with ordinary cold ham. (Not, of course, the 'processed' variety.) You need a large cantaloup melon, which you slice in half. After you have cut out the fruit, 'cubing' it with a sharp knife, you scoop round the edges of the rind, which serves as the container and looks as pretty as a piece of Chelsea china.

The great secret is the sauce. Gaskin had to work very hard to extract this from the Baron's chef, who had invented it. If he—Gaskin—had been a female he would undoubtedly have offered the chef 'liberties' for it. As it was, he procured it in exchange for a ticket to the Wembley Cup Final.

Here it is.

Mix . . . One dessertspoon of curry powder with the juice of one lemon.

Add one teaspoon of ginger, one liqueur glass of Kirsch and a sprinkling of cinnamon.

Stir these ingredients and pass through a muslin into a bowl containing a cupful of double cream with which a tablespoon of apricot purée has been blended.

Stir whole concoction briskly but do not whip. You should be able to *pour* the sauce onto the melon, rather than scoop it.

One of the virtues of this dish is that it can be used either as a very delectable first course or as a sweet at the end of dinner.

Sandwich Picasso

In the Paris of those days there lived two celebrated but obviously frustrated ladies called Gertrude Stein and Alice Toklas, who have achieved a certain fame in the history of art. I think they were totally bogus—but then, I think so many other generally accepted people and institutions nowadays are totally bogus that this opinion may carry little weight. Sometimes, groping for a descriptive phrase, I translate people into flowers. So let us say that Gertrude Stein was a very sturdy bi-sexual transatlantic hollyhock that had been planted in an alien soil. Alice Toklas was an endearing sort of weed of the convolvulus family, that had climbed up the hollyhock.

I first ate the Picasso sandwich in Gertrude Stein's studio on the morning after a quite appalling dinner which had been given for the two ladies by an American called Avery Hopwood, who was not only an atrocious dramatist but an advanced drug-addict. If you ask me how I got mixed up in such a galère, your guess is as good as mine. The dinner began with a rendezvous in the Ritz bar—the men's bar that gives onto the Rue Cambon—and when they arrived my heart sank, for the impression they gave was not bi-sexual but tri-sexual, with Hopwood in a briskly-curled toupé, Stein in a sort of smock, and Toklas crowned with a very dirty workman's cap. Where we dined I forget, but it ended with Hopwood leaning over the table and flicking open a little gold case filled with a white powder, which he offered to us. Cocaine. The with-it hard drug of the twenties. This did not appeal to me at all, nor did it appeal to Gertrude and Alice; they were suddenly transformed from bogus American careerists into frightened middle-aged ladies confronted with a cardinal sin. So I bundled them into a taxi, paid the bill, took Avery home to his hotel, undressed him, put him to bed, and went back to the Embassy. So exquisitely sensitive was the Baron that on this occasion he demanded no stories of amorous adventures. Instead, we sat back in the Louis Seize salon and sipped our Vichy water, while he regaled me with memoirs of Marcel Proust.

On the following morning I called at Gertrude Stein's studio with a large bunch of roses. They seemed the appropriate flower, for she had recently delivered herself of her most famous observation . . . 'A rose is a rose is a rose.' The fact that this mental hiccup was taken seriously, so that it rang round the world and made its way into the jargon of the contemporary intellectual banter, is a proof of the general idiocy of mankind.

The two ladies were at home, in a very battered condition. Gertrude Stein looked as though she had been feeding hens in the rain and Toklas still wore her workman's cap. I doubt if either of them had been to bed. Yes, they said, it has been too terrible, and what beautiful roses. I hoped she would say what beautiful roses-roses-roses but she did not oblige. Instead, she offered me a sandwich.

'There is only one left,' she said. 'Picasso has eaten all the others. He has just left.'

This was bitter news. To have missed Picasso was a bad mark in one's journalistic career. In one's financial career too. There were Picasso's all over the place, on the sofa, propped up against the wall, and probably in the loo. From many of them I shrank—and still do—but they all had an explosive quality which triggered off a sympathetic explosion in myself. Maybe great art does not always demand this sort of explosion, but it plays its part.

Anyway, if I had been a beady-eyed little art dealer, I should have slithered round the room, picking up scraps of paper, slipping sketches into my pockets. I might even have found a sofa cushion which was still warm with the imprint of the Master's bottom and got him to sign it. (Lot Number 173A at Sotheby's in the year 1990 and a bargain at £100,000.) As it was I sat down and prepared to tackle the sandwich which was the last thing I wanted at that hour of the morning. Miss Stein held up her hand.

'But you have not got your vodka. The sandwich was made to go with vodka. Alice, where is the vodka?'

In due course the vodka appeared. I gulped it, blinked, gulped and blinked again. The Picasso sandwich was as explosive as the Picasso pictures, and the reason I can remember the ingredients is because even in those days I was a hard-working and conscientious reporter and knew that I could get a couple of guineas for the recipe.

Here it is . . .

Take a long French roll, split it in half, wipe both halves with a clove of garlic, butter them very slightly, smear them with French mustard, and put them aside to go under the grill.

Have ready . . .

A slice of Gruyère cheese.
A handful of black olives, stoned.
Three or four rings of raw sliced onion.
Half a dozen anchovies.
Cayenne pepper.

Put the rolls under the grill on the gas stove (not too hot). When the butter has almost melted, apply the cheese and then spread on the other things. Clamp the rolls together and eat while piping hot, as though one were devouring a hot dog.

I do not know to what extent this sandwich was Picasso's standard diet, nor indeed if he ever ate it at all except to oblige Gertrude Stein. But some people may agree that it is the sort of diet which might well have sustained the man who painted *Guernica*.

Before leaving the studio I will recall another fragment of gossip from which, no doubt, I made another couple of guineas. It seems that a number of distinguished English people had recently visited the studio. Among them was Lady Diana Cooper, who has always had an affinity with the avant garde. But some of the pictures puzzled her so much that she was naïve enough —or shall we say honest enough?—to ask what they meant. This irritated Stein; one should never ask what the Master meant; meanings were for lesser mortals. So she came out with her stock reply.

'The line,' she retorted. 'Can't you appreciate the *line*?'

Lady Diana looked more closely. Then she stepped back, and gave one of her enchanting smiles.

'Of course,' she murmured. 'The lion. In the left hand corner. I can see its tail.'

CHAPTER 4

War and Peace

I HAVE lived so much of my life in public that any attempt to live it again would be a boring exercise in the dèja vu. The flash-back to the twenties was perhaps justified, in setting the stage for Gaskin's entrance, and establishing his personality. But now we must move more swiftly, waving farewell to the early years, turning into the thirties, striding towards the storm clouds.

I had a peculiar war. It was not heroic, but neither was it cosy. It involved me in such stresses that for some years afterwards I kept a revolver in the safe, to ensure that I could make a swift exit if physical pain became unbearable. One can have enough of a good thing, and one of those things is life itself. The war also showed me, at times, the funny side of death. The background for one of these revelations began on the North-West Frontier of India, in early 1943, where I had been sent, disguised as a war correspondent. I could not find any war, and suffered no inconvenience from shot or shell, but

I picked up a bug that was nearly as lethal. This involved an operation, by twilight, in a ruined fortress, with no anaesthetic but a bottle of rum. Having survived the operation, I was carried through the mountains to a converted maternity hospital and dumped in a ward reserved for dangerous murderers. They were all chained to their beds, and a nicer collection of bearded cut-throats one could not have asked for. They, too, saw the funny side of death, for though their days were num-bered, they spent their time pretending to have babies, stuffing pillows under their shirts, and jangling their fetters in simulated labour pains. From this curious establishment I was transported to Bombay, for two more operations, after which I was taken to the home of some charming Parsees who had been warned to expect a corpse. So had the nurse, who took an instant dislike to me. She used to sit outside the bedroom answering the telephone, composing bulletins about my condition. The man who seemed most interested was the head of Reuter's News Agency, who rang up about three times a day. 'No,' she would sigh, in accents of evident regret, 'Mr Nichols is not dead yet. No. He is still with us.' After a pause, in somewhat brighter tones . . . 'per-haps you would ring tomorrow, at about noon? *Then* we may have some news.'

All this, however, is anticipating, and the only reason for this brief interlude is to recall Gaskin's attitude to the hostilities, and to illustrate the manner in which the perfect manservant manages to rise above such tiresome interruptions in life.

What was one to do about him? This was the question that constantly presented itself. There was no need to ask it on my own account because, as a war correspondent, I merely did what I was told and went where I was directed—flying with the RAF, scorching with the fire-fighters, diving with the submarines, and cruising up and down the English Channel in rickety, makeshift vessels, in a state of some apprehension lest one were to meet any E-boats.

But Gaskin was a different case. At all costs, obviously, he must be protected; he must be kept intact, so that he could resume his ministrations when the prevailing lunacies had exhausted themselves. This respite, presumably, would not be long delayed, for in those early days we were constantly assured, on the highest authority, that the war could not possibly last longer than a few months. In the meantime, how was he to be suitably preserved? Admittedly, he had varicose veins, but they were not very bad ones, though they looked worse when he was wearing the expensive silk socks which I had rashly given him as a Christmas present. But one could not ask him to go hobbling about the place in silk socks merely to avoid 'doing his bit'. That would be definitely unpatriotic.

But what *was* his 'bit'? Knowing him so well, I had definite views on that question. His 'bit' was to cosset somebody like Lord Montgomery, producing exquisite soufflés on the desert sands, and daintily removing any small portions of shrapnel that might have coarsened the texture of the dish if Rommel had been in the neighbourhood. Or Mountbatten. He would have been splendid with Mountbatten, who personified all his conceptions of the aristocracy. If he had been with Mountbatten he would have been sure, from time to time, to run into Noël Coward, who had a 'tendre' for him, as they used to say in the Regency days. Noël sometimes had servant problems, and during one of these periods he made tentative efforts to lure Gaskin into his orbit, though never behind my back.

'Dear Gaskin,' he once sighed to me. 'Quite impossible, I imagine, to seduce?'

'Quite.'

'Even if I filled the house with cats?'

'Even if you did just that.'

'Even if I wrote a part for him in a comedy?'

Gaskin, I suggested, was quite capable of writing his own comedy, and playing it too.

But life wrote it for him. One day he received a 'calling-up notice', or whatever one calls those sinister scraps of paper that whirl about in times of war, summoning men to deadly destinations. He had brought it up on the breakfast-tray, and slipped it into the toast-rack. For a few moments it escaped my attention, because I was scarcely awake, having spent a somewhat disturbed night in a barge on the Thames, writing a story about the balloon barrage. It was called *The Balloon Boys* with a sub-title 'Unsung Heroes of the Blitz', and, so the editor later assured me, had brought tears to countless eyes.

Then I saw the piece of paper in the toast-rack.

'What is this, Gaskin?'

He gave a very Jeeves' reply. 'It would seem, sir, that my services are required in Wales.'

A brief glance confirmed this remarkable piece of information. He was ordered to report to Llandudno, in the space of forty-eight hours.

No explosion, no incendiary bomb, could have so swiftly shattered my illusions about the phoney war. Life, in the space of a second, had suddenly become odiously real and earnest, and seemed likely to become more so.

'But why Wales? There are no hostilities in Wales. Do you know anybody in Wales?'

'No, sir. Except, of course, Sir Michael Duff.'

This was impressive, but impractical. Michael Duff—one of the largest landowners in Wales—had occasionally come to dinner, but his only concourse with Gaskin had been to congratulate him on his crêpes suzette.

'I don't think we could very well approach Sir Michael.'

'Certainly not, sir.'

I struggled out of bed. One would think better after a bath. And perhaps one would be able to pull a few strings.

But I am not a very good string-puller and in this case the opportunities for string-pulling were limited. I knew a number of persons in high places, but one could scarcely summon them from Cabinet meetings to bend their attention to Gaskin's problem. How would one phrase the question? 'Could you possibly do something about a superb manservant who does not want to go to Wales and has varicose veins and makes the most delicious crêpes suzette?' No. It was not on.

Two nights later, Gaskin went to Wales. I drove him to the blacked-out station, and saw him into a crowded third-class carriage filled with young conscripts singing bawdy songs. Then I went home to an empty house, locked up his room, laid my own breakfast tray and fed the cats. Maybe I am making a great deal of fuss about nothing. It might have been worse; we might all have been blown up; and at that very moment the Germans might have been striding down the street, singing the Horst Wessel song. Even so, it was bad enough, and I felt that a chapter in my life—a very pleasant chapter— had closed for ever.

Six weeks passed, illuminated by a single letter from Gaskin which told its own story. They had ordered him to scrub floors, and then, when there was no more scrubbing to be done, to dig trenches. Why anybody should think that the war effort was being furthered by getting a Jeeves to dig trenches in the remote Welsh mountains was a problem I never endeavoured to solve.

Then one night I went up to London to dine at the Café Royal. Sitting in a corner was Oliver Messel,* looking extremely depressed. I asked him why.

* Although of recent years ill-health has limited the exercise of Oliver Messel's genius, his previous work—in the theatre, the opera, the ballet, and the cinema, as a portrait-painter, an illustrator, and a dynamic on the European aesthetic scene—has assured him of a permanent place in the history of our century.

'Tomorrow I am being sent into the wilds,' he said.
'Why?'
'To be a camouflage officer.'
'Poor Oliver! But I am sure you will do it beautifully. What sort of wilds? Not Wales, by any chance?'
'Wales? No. Why should anybody want to do camouflage in Wales?'
'I cannot imagine. But that is where they have just sent Gaskin.'

A long nostalgic sigh. 'Dear Gaskin. Darling Gaskin. Those crêpes suzette!' A sudden, sharp, beady look. 'Didn't Gaskin come from Norwich?'

'He certainly did. He knows everybody in Norwich.' (The lady in the fish shop, for example, whom Gaskin had met, years ago, on his first night in London.) 'But what has Norwich got to do with it?'

'Norwich has everything to do with it. That is where they are sending me. I am going to be a Captain. And I am going to be given an assistant, who will have to be in uniform. Gaskin would be ideal.'

'I don't think he knows anything about camouflage.'

'Nor do I. But I have marvellous ideas.' For a few moments he expounded upon those ideas, which were indeed thrilling, though perhaps they were more fitted to provide the scenic background for an outdoor ballet than to serve as a deterrent to the German fleet. Then he reverted to Gaskin. He must have him. He would teach him everything that he knew and a great deal that he did not. Without Gaskin he would refuse to camouflage anything at all. Not even a sausage.

There and then, we began to plan. Gaskin, somehow or other, must be extricated from Wales and transported to Norwich. How such an intricate exercise was to be conducted in the teeth of the enemy, I could not remotely conceive. It was worse than D-day. But Oliver triumphed. I think that he saw the whole situation—the war, the enemy, his own acceptance of this totally unexpected role, and of course, Gaskin—as an artistic challenge. His whole professional life had trained him to deal with this sort of situation. In the old days, at the eleventh hour, when the police were clearing the pavements outside Covent Garden to ensure the unimpeded progress of the Queen, he could have been observed on the top of a ladder, slashing a last slodge of shocking pink onto the back cloth. Or pinning a final scarlet carnation to the curtains of the royal box. Or ripping off a jarring ribbon from the corsage of the première ballerina. If she had been indisposed he would doubtless have volunteered to dance the role himself. Compared with such crises the transfer of Gaskin was a minor problem and in a few days he solved it.

Here is Gaskin's first war letter to me which, with a pleasing sense of irony, he had written on official paper marked Top Secret.

Dear Sir,

I am taking up my pen to thank you for arranging my transfer. It was very sudden and the General seemed very surprised.

Captain Messel is very kind to me and we get on very well and I hope I give satisfaction, though the hours are difficult as the Captain gets his best ideas after midnight. At the moment I am gluing green feathers to wire netting which will be used for putting over gun sites on the coast. From the sea the Captain says it will look like grass. He is also making designs for statues which will be used in the event of an Invasion.

The Captain sends his kindest regards and thinks you should come up and write an Article which, I hope, Sir, you may find convenient, and as I have Friends here I shall be sending some eggs which I hope will be Acceptable.

I was very glad about your getting Places for the

Cats and I hope Sir that you are Managing, with best wishes from

Yours very truly

R. A. Gaskin

In its way, this endearing epistle might be regarded as a minuscule footnote to the social history of the Great War. Or at least—if that sounds too large a claim—to the history of the use of camouflage in the defence of beleaguered nations. In spite of the amateur and almost excessively 'British' nature of the Messel–Gaskin relationship—the artistic genius of the one married to the domestic genius of the other—it does happen to be a fact that many of Oliver's ideas were widely adopted (not always with acknowledgement), during the final stages of hostilities.

One of these ideas was so bizarre perhaps that it deserves a paragraph of its own. He showed it to me on the occasion of my visit to Norwich shortly after the arrival of Gaskin's letter. It was the sketch of a small iron building, painted pale green with touches of gold, in the mid-Victorian style. It was very delicate and pretty, and at first I took it to be some sort of summer-house, or band-stand. Not at all, said Oliver; it was intended to be a gentlemen's lavatory. But how would such an object serve the cause of the Allies, I enquired; and where would it be erected, and who would use it, and with what effect? The Germans would use it, he replied, in the early stages of the Invasion. After a protracted voyage across the North Sea they would feel the need of some such convenience. Besides, they would be under orders to behave with decorum and to do nothing which would alarm the inhabitants. Therefore, when they saw this welcoming little building, standing by the side of the road on one of the main entrances to the city, they would naturally wish to avail themselves of its services. And as soon as they stepped inside, it would instantly explode.

I do not know, and rather doubt, whether this ingenious apparatus was ever put to practical use.

I was not often able to visit Norwich, owing to the aforesaid activities as a war correspondent, but every time I did so I was greatly refreshed. Oliver was doing a vital job, but somehow one had the feeling that he regarded it as an exceptionally difficult assignment in the ballet rather than as a part of the war effort. He worked very hard indeed, reaching the peak of his inspiration, as Gaskin had warned me, at about midnight. (Gaskin, by the way, had been promoted soon after arrival, because the Powers that Be, for some reason best known to themselves had decided to give him the rank of Bombardier Sergeant. In my private opinion this was a most unsuitable title, suggesting the roar of guns and the smoke of battle, but Gaskin was delighted with it, and used it on every possible occasion. When he lifted the receiver to answer the telephone he invariably announced himself with the words 'Bombardier Gaskin speaking'. He adopted a rather snooty accent, pronouncing it 'Bombadyeah'. He made it sound so impressive that sometimes the people at the other end—particularly if they were artists, as they often were—assumed that he must be some sort of general and promptly called him 'sir'.)

The refreshment which I gained from these visits to Norwich was not only mental but physical. Gaskin's local friends were mostly drawn from the farming community, and often lavished him with presents of eggs, butter, and vegetables. With these he worked his familiar miracles, which were greatly appreciated by the higher-ranking officers, who—when offered a dinner beginning with a spinach omelette, progressing to chicken à la Kiev stuffed with butter, followed by fresh peaches with clotted cream and ending up with a particularly delectable variety of angels on horseback—seemed to develop a convenient blindness to the fact that they were consuming, in the space of one hour, the equivalent of one month's ration allowance for a working-class family of six. I suppose that I should have had moral qualms, but I hadn't. The working-class families would have behaved in precisely the same manner, if they had been given the opportunity. Nobody in Britain suffered serious privations during the war; indeed, compared with the Germans, ours was quite a cosy conflict. All the same, the rich were obviously cushioned against any major culinary discomforts.

Flash forward. Dining with Maggie Greville at the Dorchester in the last month of hostilities. For a moment I must be a gossip writer—(no crime, if the gossip is good)—and mention that Maggie was the Honourable Mrs Ronald Greville, one of the last great Edwardian hostesses, fabulously rich, and a great entertainer of royalty. One day, the then Archbishop of Canterbury rather rashly reminded her that she should not put her trust in princes. 'I never do,' she replied sweetly. 'I merely ask them to dinner.'

Flash back. Dinner at the Dorchester that night was quite dramatic. Bombs all over the place. Bang, bang, bang. The wail of syrens punctuating the conversation. But in Maggie's suite—stretching across half a floor—an artificial calm prevailed, which was reflected in the impassive countenance of Bowles the butler, Bacon the under-butler, and Hawkins the first footman, who were always brought up from the country when she was giving a dinner-party. The food was delicious as in the days of peace, but Maggie was at pains to assure us that everything was strictly in accordance with the rationing regulations. 'I abhor the black market,' she told us, helping herself to a large dollop of caviar, explaining as she did so that it was a gift from the dear American Ambassador. And we need have no guilty consciences about the cream, because it came from her home farm where the cows, apparently, were producing too much of it, so that it had to be used up. 'I abhor waste,' she proclaimed. The comble came with what I took to be a chicken mousse. This was the pièce de resistance in more senses than one. 'Tell me, Beverley dear, what do you think of my little mousse?' I began to murmur that it was delicious, but she said . . . 'No, dear Beverley, what do you think is *in* it?' I had just swallowed some of the salad—(iced hothouse grapes sprinkled with slices of fresh tarragon)—so I had to have another taste. 'Well, obviously,' I began, 'there are truffles.' But Maggie was not interested in the truffles. Of course there were truffles, but that was not the point. The vital ingredient—and now she turned to the assembled company with a green and glittering gesture—(she was wearing the Greville emeralds because the bank charged such a monstrous rate of interest and anyway, if one were going to be blown up one might as well be blown up in the style to which one had been accustomed)—the vital ingredient was . . . pause . . . bang, bang, bang . . . *Rabbit!* Silence. Bang, bang, bang. As we reverted to this melting concoction we had a curious feeling that by consuming it we were giving proof of our patriotism and our capacity for self-sacrifice. And perhaps it was ungenerous of me to notice that at the moment when Maggie made her dramatic announcement her eyes had turned, ever so casually, towards the wife of the Chilean Ambassador, whom she detested. The shoulders of this lady were draped in a variety of fur which by no stretch of the imagination could have been mistaken for silver mink.

We can now return to Gaskin, Oliver, and the harsh realities of the war.

Although Gaskin, as we have noted, was usually able to cushion Oliver against the major culinary discomforts of this painful period there were times when even he was at a loss. One of these occurred shortly after the visit of a high-ranking officer for whose delectation he had rashly prepared a succulent dish of duckling. The officer, far from being delighted, was shocked; and even in the piping days of peace he would have regarded such a dish with disapproval. In times of war, it was an outrage. Oliver was severely ticked off. I would like to have been present on this occasion, which must have had an element of high comedy . . . the general, blustering round the crowded studio, Oliver, endeavouring to look 'military'. He must have looked about as 'military' as Nyjinski in the last sequences of *L'Après Midi*. Even on the rare occasions when I saw him standing to attention he gave the impression that he was poised for an entrechat.

However, he got the message, and when the general had gone, he asked Gaskin to join him for a drink.

'Dear Bombardier,' he said, 'I don't think we should have any more duck.'

Gaskin raised his eyebrows. 'Was there anything amiss, sir?'

'No. It was superb. But we have to think of the rationing coupons. The general said so.'

'Coupons' was not Gaskin's favourite word. I think that he had a touch of French blood, and when the French are confronted by tiresome regulations, particularly if they are concerned with the pleasures of the table, they have a genius for evading them. Besides, in this case, the duckling had been presented to him by the widow of a prosperous inn-keeper who, I fancy, 'had her eye on him'. So it seemed a little unfair that he should be reproved, and if he had not been the perfect manservant he might have sulked, and taken offence. Instead, he stepped at once into the role of Jeeves.

'In that case, sir,' he observed, setting down his empty glass, 'I imagine that we must content ourselves with Spam?'

For the moment Oliver did not seem to hear him. He was bent over a canvas, putting the finishing touches to the navel of a Baroque cherub, which was to be erected—rendered in plaster—in the Market Square. The navel was the most important part of the design because it was to conceal the muzzle of a machine gun which would belch death and destruction at the enemy.

'Spam,' repeated Oliver vaguely. 'Dear Bombardier, that would be delicious.'

And it was.

SPAM A LA GASKIN

Spam is still with us, in various guises. It lurks on the cheaper shelves of Sainsbury's, and Marks and Sparks, with pretty pink labels, printed in Denmark or Holland, informing us that it contains . . .

Pork, Pork Stock, Edible Starch, Casein, Salt, Spices, Emulsifying Salts, Potassium Nitrate, Sodium Nitrate, Permitted Colour.

These ingredients, one would have thought, would be quite enough to provide us with acute stomach troubles for the rest of our lives, particularly the 'permitted colour'. What this means is anybody's guess. To me it suggests a girl in a factory-line with her hands clutching some sort of squeezing device, wondering if she is squirting in too much carmine.

Spam *à la nature* could hardly be described as a festive dish, but Gaskin transformed it into something that one would not have spurned at the Ritz. I still have the recipe which I took home with me from Norwich. As usual, with his charming sense of irony, he had transcribed it on paper headed Top Secret. And in his memory a secret it shall remain.

CHAPTER 5

A Touch of the East

GASKIN has held the centre of the stage for long enough and it is time that he stepped into the wings. For we have now reached the penultimate year of the war, when I was despatched to India, for reasons which may have been clear to the authorities but were never apparent to anybody else.

As previously hinted, my role in the hostilities was not heroic but neither was it comfortable. This was evident during the voyage out. I had an idea that they might be sending me to report on the Burma campaign, which was hotting up, so it seemed prudent to ask the Ministry of Information what clothes would be required. With misplaced irony I quipped . . . 'I suppose that I shall scarcely be needing a dinner-jacket?' On the contrary, they replied, a dinner-jacket was essential. This was unexpected, but it suggested a good story. Fixing one's black tie in a hail of bullets, shaking cobras from one's silk socks. It would read very well in the Sundays. Then I said, 'Should I take something warm?' They scoffed at this suggestion. 'You are going to *India*,' they reminded me, 'by convoy through the Mediterranean. Within three days of embarkation you will be walking round the deck in shorts.'

But it was not to be quite like that. Three weeks after embarkation I was shivering on the deck of an ancient oil-tanker which had come to a halt in a dense fog outside the coasts of Newfoundland. Because of a sudden flurry of U-boat activity the convoy had been diverted across the Atlantic. Six of our ships had already been sunk. To guard against the cold my thin tropical suit was heavily padded with old copies of the *News of the World*, kindly supplied by the radio operator, who afterwards committed suicide. If ever a man had reason for doing so, he had, for his job was to sit in his little office, translating messages of death from ships within calling distance. I used to sit there with him for lack of anything better to do. 'U-boat sighted. U-boat drawing close. U-boat within range. Abandoning ship.' Or words to that effect. And then, silence.

I often wonder how Gaskin would have behaved in this situation. That he would have risen above it, by some miracle of organization, I have no doubt. The happiest solution might have been if we had all been sunk and captured, and if he had endeared himself to the Captain and cooked such delicious meals for the crew that they would all have eaten themselves to death.

From Gaskin to Hussein. From the immaculate blue pin-stripe of a gentleman's gentleman to the floppy white trousers and rakish turban of the sahib's 'bearer'. From the rain-swept lawn of an English cottage to the sun-scorched roof of a Bombay bungalow. And—for the professed purposes of this volume—from crèpes suzette to curry, a dish which Hussein prepared with the touch of a master.

The tribulations of my Indian adventure have been

described in a previous volume,* which still evokes hisses of hatred from senior members of the Hindu Congress. It covers a wide range of the Indian scene—religious, political, economic, social, aesthetic—which has changed only slightly in its fundamentals during the past thirty years, and it was only recently, when I reopened it, that I realized that one essential figure was missing from the panorama—Hussein.

He was a strapping Pathan from the North-West, over six foot, of great strength and endurance. This was fortunate because later, when things got bad, he was often obliged to carry me in his arms when no other form of transport was available. I engaged him, against everybody's advice, because of an endearing remark which he made when he came to be interviewed. He had produced from one of his capacious pockets a tattered bundle of 'references'. These were difficult to interpret, as most of them were written in Urdu. Apart from that, they were plentifully interlarded with advertisements for aphrodisiacs, of which—judging from his subsequent conduct—he stood in no immediate need. Making little of this hotchpotch I asked him the profession of his previous employer.

'He very good sahib,' replied Hussein. 'He captain in army and navy.'

Hussein, evidently, had the makings of an Indian Jeeves, and I engaged him on the spot.

A few days later we were summoned to stay with the Viceroy, the Marquess of Linlithgow, whose courage and foresight in one of the world's most difficult situations has not yet been recognized by historians. I had heard much about the pomp and circumstance of the Viceregal Lodge, which apparently exceeded the splendour of Buckingham Palace, but I felt reasonably equipped because of the aforesaid dinner-jacket. Hussein was a different case. He looked very scruffy indeed, his baggy

* *Verdict on India*, Jonathan Cape, 1944.

white trousers were badly cut, his tunic was patched, and he needed a hair cut.

I told him to attend to these things, and gave him the money to pay for them, assuming that he would go to some tailor who specialized in making uniforms for officers' bearers. Instead, he immediately went on a buying spree in the bazaars, and returned late at night looking like something out of an early Diaghileff ballet, with décor by Bakst. His white trousers gleamed in the moonlight. A golden sash encircled his slender waist. His scarlet tunic recalled the ceremonial uniform of the Brigade of Guards. As if this were not enough, he had plastered it with decorations.

'But Hussein, where did you get all those medals?'

'In bazaar, sahib. Very cheap.'

'But what *are* they?'

He pointed to them with a dark sinewy thumb. 'This one German, sahib. Very cheap. Two rupee. This one Chinese, sahib. Fifty anna. Real silver. This one . . .' he shrugged his shoulders.

'And that one?' I was looking at a little token of bronze, hanging on a faded ribbon. His lips parted in a brilliant smile.

'That one, sahib, Victoria Cross.'

And so it proved to be. When we eventually arrived at the Viceregal Lodge, in a glittering cavalcade, all the other important personages—ambassadors, field marshals, admirals, and what-have-you—were accompanied by bearers in sober black and white, who stared at Hussein with considerable disapproval. *They* were serving masters of far greater eminence, and it seemed unfair that they should not be permitted similar marks of distinction. But Lady Linlithgow was enchanted, though she suggested that perhaps we had better keep Hussein away from any of the more touchy Maharajas. 'I have a feeling,' she said, 'that they would feel somewhat underdressed.'

And so, for the next year, in a long-drawn-out tragi-comedy, which I will not recapitulate, Hussein was constantly at my side, trudging in the wake of stretchers, sitting by my bed-side, carrying me up staircases and—when at last I could sit up and take nourishment—concocting his delicious curries.

And always, in the background, walked the shadow of Gaskin.

In a volume so discursive as this, the occasional pause for thought is not only permissible but obligatory. I should like to say a word about the master–servant relationship. It is not readily comprehended by the present generation, to whom 'service' is a dirty word. Perhaps this is hardly surprising; not so very long ago 'service' was a dirty job, grossly underpaid, and generally despised. The cold winter mornings of my youth still carry the memory of housemaids kneeling on the hearth rug raking out the ashes from the grate while I lay in bed, staring at them with eyes which, I would like to think, showed a hint of sympathy. It was the same in the higher ranks of society. I remember a hot summer evening in the thirties when I called at a rather splendid house in London to escort a lady to a dinner party which was being given on the other side of the square. Her name was Lady Juliet Duff, and she was one of the most intelligent, sensitive, and witty women of her generation. But she had a blind spot about servants. When we emerged from the house to go to the party, her car was waiting to drive us across the square. At the wheel was a young chauffeur, of striking good looks, sweating in his smart uniform. He was an ardent, restless, male human being who at that moment should have been lying on the grass under a tree in Hyde Park, clad in something loose, with his arm round an equally ardent and restless female human being, clad in something looser. But no. When I suggested that since it was such a beautiful evening we might walk—two hundred yards—and dismiss the chauffeur, Lady Juliet did not seem to hear. And when, a minute later, we arrived at the party, she required him—with the utmost charm, to be waiting to drive us back across the square at ten o'clock. 'But Juliet, isn't that rather early?' To which she replied, 'One never knows. We may be bored.' It was midnight before we left, and sure enough the young chauffeur was waiting. He was sweating more than ever, for the night was hotting up, and a fire was smouldering in his eyes.

Such trivia form the fabric of revolution. Well, the revolution has arrived, and we are paying the price for it.

With Hussein, as the long last year of the war went by, and as he accompanied me on my erratic and usually painful progress through the sub-continent, there were no such complications. I was the sahib and he was the bearer, and that was how God, or rather Allah, had ordained it. Frankly, I began to get rather bored with Allah, who was always popping up with some new physical torment. Apart from that, Allah, according to Hussein, held very reactionary ideas about the master-servant relationship. Wherever we stayed, in bungalows, hospitals, government houses, flats, and still more hospitals, we were attended by slaves of the 'sweeper' class, who were regarded by the majority of Indians as 'untouchable'. (And still are, whatever Mrs Gandhi may have to say about it.) For these, Hussein had neither patience nor pity. He chased them, and kicked them, and smacked them, and nothing that I could say or do had the least effect upon him. These wretched creatures, scrubbing the floors and emptying the dustbins, were only to be despised, and even if the shadow of one of them fell across my plate he would snatch it from the table and throw it away.

'But Hussein, what have they done? Why are you so beastly to them? Why did you throw that plate away?'

'If sahib eat food from that plate . . .' His vocabulary

was inadequate to describe the degradations which would ensue.

'But, *why*?'

'It is the will of Allah.'

If I were in the habit of using four-letter words I could have suggested, very tersely, what somebody might have done to Allah at such moments.

Not for the first time, I sighed for Gaskin, who had no religion, and was a better cook. Apart from the afore-mentioned curry, to which we will at last revert.

The Indian adventure ended, as it had begun, in the Viceregal Lodge at Delhi. Needless to say, there has been no Burma campaign, and no opportunity to discover how one would have behaved in the heat of battle. (Oddly enough, in moments of extreme crisis, one usually behaves rather better than would have been expected.) I was a wiser and very much thinner man. From 154 pounds I had shrunk to a rather tottery 112, and Hussein spent much of his spare time sitting cross-legged on the floor taking in my trousers. He also spent some time modifying his own uniform, because the new Vice-roy, Lord Wavell, was a distinguished soldier, who might have been unamused if he had seen me arriving accompanied by a bearer decorated with the Victoria Cross.

Too often, when we walk with history we have little sense that history is being made. How are we to guess that the quiet street where we sat drinking our wine is soon to be swept by the tides of revolution? That the flames are soon to destroy some ancient house where we stayed a few days ago? That death has already set his mark on the great man whose hand we have so recently shaken?

But now, in this farewell visit to Delhi, as I stepped out into the brilliantly patterned gardens of the last and greatest of our imperial palaces—we were dining out-of-doors—there was no need to be reminded that one was 'walking with history'. It was in the air one breathed, it was written in the star-dusted sky. Every country in the world has a different sky, which mirrors the personality of its people as clearly as the sky of a painter reflects the personality of the artist. The most striking evidence of this is to be seen in Israel, and particularly in Jerusalem. When you climb the Mount of Olives you feel that if you stood on tiptoe you could touch the sky—a climatic-psychological phenomenon which may explain why this part of the world has given birth to so many of the world's great religious leaders. But in India it was always different, and tonight it was more different than it had ever been. There was no question of touching the sky with your fingers; it was far, far away, and it was drifting further. India was vanishing from the Imperial orbit; even the most distant stars were deserting us. And yet, the Imperial pageant went on.

Dinner was served.

As we sat at the long table all my senses were keenly alert. For the sense of smell there was the perfume of tuberoses; for the sense of sound the mystic chorus of crickets. For the sense of sight there were a hundred stimulations; the sparkle of the women's saris in the candlelight, the bold primary colours of the men's uniforms, the heaped piles of scarlet hibiscus scattered down the length of the table, all against a staccato scintillating dance of fireflies. But there was another sense—a social sense, if one may so describe it, and it was sharpened by fear. This array of pomp and circumstance was marching to a sombre background. Though the lawns were green and freshly watered, the Imperial terrain was cracking all around us; though the thunders of war were far distant, we could still hear them, in our minds, mingling with the thunder from the hills. And though we had dined well, there was famine in the land, and hatred in the air. The curtain of Empire was falling and the mob was waiting in the wings.

It was then that Wavell rose to his feet and proposed the toast of the King Emperor. And it was then that there came from the darkness the sound of the bagpipes, and into the circle of light around us there swung a troop of kilted highlanders, the men of his own regiment, the Black Watch. They marched round the table three times, making their fiery music, while all of us, white, black, off-white, stood to attention thinking our separate thoughts. Maybe they were among the thoughts that lie too deep for tears, and I will not bore the reader with my own reflections. But when I set down my glass I was weeping, and with no shame at all.

Among the senses that were stimulated on this emotional occasion I mentioned those of sound and scent and sight—the chirruping crickets, the languorous tuberoses and the sparkling uniforms. But there was another sense, equally vivid, with no aesthetic vibrations—the sense of taste. Which brings us back to business.

The sense of taste was provided by an exquisite curry, in which I recognized the unique touch of Hussein. History was repeating itself. Just as Gaskin had tried out his skill in the kitchen of the Norwegian Embassy, in Paris twenty years ago, so Hussein was weaving his spells in the kitchens of the Viceroy at the present moment. Of this there could be no doubt whatever, because the first of the many side-dishes that were being handed round was his own speciality which I have never encountered in any Western country—a form of paste made from fresh limes, which was at once delicate and stinging.

I greatly admired Hussein that night for his persistence in master-minding this curry, because he must have been up against a great deal of competition. How many chefs served in the Viceregal kitchens? I do not know. Nor, presumably, will anybody else ever know, for this is the sort of fascinating detail that imperial historians are inclined to ignore. How many servants waited at table?

I have no idea. All I can recall is a general impression of dusky white-clad figures hovering in the darkness, as in some exotic ballet, of white-gloved hands proffering dishes of gold and silver and bronze, from which there drifted a blend of subtle aromas, bitter and sweet and sharp and soft and sour. If Oscar Wilde had ever stayed with our Indian Viceroy—an occasion which would have inspired Max Beerbohm to a charming vignette—he might have composed a tapestry of prose as rich as any of those which smoulder in the pages of *Dorian Gray*. But then Oscar, alas, never wrote a cookery book, though he made an epigram which might deservedly have sparkled on the title page . . . 'Even the cardinal virtues will not atone for half-cold entrées.'

Hussein's Curry Recipe

This is perhaps a misleading title, for Hussein's role in the recipe is confined to the trimmings. It would have been a waste of time to clutter these pages with the standard curry procedures, which do not greatly vary, and are reprinted year after year in cookery books and women's magazines. Somebody once observed that 'History repeats itself and historians repeat one another.' This is even truer of cooks and cookery correspondents.

But there were some things about Hussein's technique which—to me at any rate—were new. The most important was that instead of using a tin of ordinary curry powder he always made his own mixture. There was no need for him to do so because, even in those days of shortages, there were shops in Bombay where one could find most of the luxuries which had long vanished from the cities of Europe.

But Hussein would have none of this. Instead, he used to go to the bazaars and return with little bags of herbs and spices which he laid out on the floor and proceeded to pound in a cracked china bowl which bore the unlikely inscription of 'A Present from Blackpool'. It was decorated by the portraits of two bright blue mermaids, with immense bosoms. From time to time, he would pause in his work, lift up the bowl, and stroke these images with an appreciative thumb.

'Where did you get that bowl, Hussein?'

'The English captain give me, sahib. Before you come.'

'The captain who was in the army and navy?'

'Yes, sahib. He says bowl very valuable.'

Sometimes I used to wonder if the English captain had a touch of Hindu blood.

Hussein's curry mixture can be reproduced with reasonable accuracy, thanks to the kindly attention of various British memsahibs, who from time to time used to cluster round my sick bed, taking notes. Here it is.

3 tablespoonsful powdered ginger, ground pepper, cumin and coriander.

1 tablespoonful crushed chillies, turmeric and fenugreek.

1 teaspoonful of cloves.

(All these are 'readily obtainable at oriental stockists' . . . if you use that sort of language.)

There was one mystery ingredient whose composition he never revealed to me. It was a white powder and he used to sprinkle a pinch of it over the Blackpool bowl as a finishing touch. As he did so he would turn his head in the direction of one of the younger British memsahibs, and bestow upon her a suggestive wink. But he never disclosed the nature of the powder. For all we know it may have been only bicarbonate of soda. And yet, when I remember all those tattered advertisements for aphrodisiacs which he produced from among his references on our first interview, I wonder. At any rate, it seemed to cheer me up.*

* It was only some time after these words were written that I discovered that Constance Spry had published a recipe, in her own

To me, curries are essentially fun dishes. (Unless one is mad enough to buy those ready-made-up packages from the supermarkets, which are advertised as coming from China but have obviously been imported hot from hell.) You can put almost anything into them—fish, fowl, or good red-herring, fruit, vegetables, shell-fish. And, of course, left-overs. You can serve them hot or cold. You can make them on Monday and eat them on Tuesday. And whatever the weather, they seem to adapt themselves to the occasion.

Cookery Book, for something very like Hussein's home-made mixture. However, she tones down the quantities of hot herbs and complicates the process by adding cardamon seed and poppy seed, both of which, in these days, are hard to come by.

CHAPTER 6

Country Gentleman

ON the outbreak of peace Gaskin returned from the war more of a snob than ever.

Perhaps 'returned from the war' is an unduly heroic way of putting it; in fact he only returned from Norwich, with a very plump duck in his kit bag. And one must admit that the role ordained for him during the conflict had not involved any special ardours nor endurances. Compared with some people's wars, his had been a picnic. A subject on which we need not enlarge, because other people's wars are almost as boring as other people's babies.

The first thing we did was to have a drink together. This sounds a simple statement, but in the ingredients of that drink and in the way he served it the whole Jeeves' mystique was typified.

I suddenly found myself confronted with a silver tray, a cocktail shaker—misted with cold—and a glass.

'I thought you might care for a Sidecar, sir.'

'A Sidecar?'

Even from Gaskin, this was an astonishing suggestion. The ingredients of this nostalgic cocktail are Cointreau, liqueur brandy and fresh lemon juice. How had he discovered these things—particularly the lemons—in wartime Norwich? Perhaps it was wiser not to enquire.

I asked him to sit down. Another simple statement but a modern Gaskin, if such a phenomenon were imaginable, would probably have sat down without being asked, and in the best chair. And the way in which he disposed himself suggested the dexterity of a practised light comedy actor—tray deftly placed on side-table, cocktail poured out with a single gesture, seating posture comfortable but upright.

We drank each other's health. There was a moment's awkward pause, for we were both thinking of the same thing. He broke the silence with perfect tact.

'May I assume, sir, that you will wish me to return?'

'Of course. Why do you ask?'

'There have been various Offers, sir.'

I could well believe it. A great many officers had passed through Norwich and they could hardly have failed to be impressed by Gaskin's capabilities.

'What sort of offers?'

'None of them was at all suitable. One of the generals was very persistent but when I met his wife I knew that it would not Do. Not at all a lady, sir. If it comes to that, quite a number of the officers were not what we would call the Thing.'

'In what way, Gaskin?'

'Table manners, sir. For example, the port.'

'What about the port?'

'They seemed to be unfamiliar with the normal procedure.'

This was indeed a startling revelation of the secret history of the higher ranks of the British army in the last days of the war.

'You mean . . . they passed it the wrong way round?'

'Precisely, sir.'

'What did Captain Messel say?'

'The Captain never noticed things like that.'

'What else?'

'Manners of speech, sir. One could not help overhearing things. There was an occasion when a major in quite a good regiment referred to Lady Diana Cooper as "Lady Di". That sort of thing. And very few of them seemed to know how to address myself. Either they were too familiar or they treated me as though we were on parade.'

He rose to his feet, without being asked. His timing was perfect.

'At what hour will you be requiring dinner?'

The old familiar question sounded as sweet as music, particularly as a duck was looming in the background.

'Shall we say eight o'clock?'

'Thank you, sir.' At the door he paused and looked back. 'If I may say so, you look as though you need Feeding Up.'

Although I called him a snob the word is misleading. It would be truer to describe him as a romantic. And although he was happy in my service he should really have been head of a large household in a stately home. He always reminded me of the butler in Punch, opening the door to a scruffy little agitator who announced that the revolution had arrived. 'The revolution?' repeated the butler haughtily. 'Kindly deliver it at the servant's entrance.'

Consider the case of Merry Hall, the large country house where we were soon to take up residence. I have already sketched the adventures of Merry Hall in a trilogy of books,* but as these were partly fictional I never made clear the fact that it was largely because of

* Republished in 1972 under the title of *The Gift of a Home*, W. H. Allen.

Gaskin that I ever went there at all. It was he who discovered the advertisement in *The Times*, and he fell in love with the title. His first remark, before he had even seen it, was that 'Merry Hall would look nice on the notepaper'.

And when he did see it, and when we went down to explore its twenty-two rooms, with their conservatories and cellars and attics and rambling outbuildings, instead of being indignant that he should be expected to run such a place single-handed, he was enchanted. The larger the better. His kitchen was gigantic—the sort of baronial kitchen in which Cinderella is revealed by the fireplace in the first act. This, he observed calmly, would give him 'room to move around'. The cellars stretched under the entire house and some of them looked as though their roofs were about to collapse. This deterred him not at all, for in one of them he discovered a room lined with dusty shelves which still bore the painted enamel labels of the wines they had once carried . . . Madeira, Brandy, Claret, Burgundy, Hock, Port, Sauternes, Tokay . . . and still more Madeira. A modern servant confronted by such an array would have gaped, or smouldered with revolutionary thoughts, and in either case probably demanded a rise in salary. Gaskin's reaction was to sweep the labels deftly into his handkerchief, observing that they could 'do with a good scrub'. And then to turn to me, saying 'I have always felt, sir, that we should have a nice cellar.' So, quite frankly, had I. The only problem had been what I could afford to put in it.

In spite of all the chaos of moving into a house four times larger than we had ever occupied in the past, the cuisine was uninterrupted. Delicious meals served in the Georgian dining room—still largely unfurnished—on spotless plates with sparkling silver, at precisely the hour appointed. Gaskin was like my Yorkshire grandmother, who once reprimanded a housemaid in a single chilling sentence, 'When I say breakfast at eight, I do not mean breakfast at one minute *past* eight.' He was never one minute past anything. When luncheon was announced, one put down the pen, rose from the desk, and walked obediently to the dining room—even if one were in the grip of a strong emotion or in the middle of a passage of felicitous dialogue. Maybe, without his flawless perfectionism I should have written better prose.

Yes, the cooking went on, but it began to assume a different flavour. A country flavour.

For the first time in my life I had an enormous kitchen garden. Well, it was over an acre which should be enough for anybody unless one proposed to run a vegetarian boarding-house, and it had been superbly stocked and tended by a rugged old Yorkshireman called Oldfield. He had only one eye, but he saw more with that eye than most men see with two.

There were so many other areas to explore on the estate that it was several weeks before I even noticed the asparagus beds. There were three, each about forty feet long, and they were breaking out all over into a forest of fat green stalks. At last, one would have enough asparagus, or rather too much, for asparagus is one of those delicacies which, like oysters and caviar, demands to be consumed in excess. Half a dozen oysters, or a spoonful of caviar merely act as an irritation to the palate, and eight spindly stalks of asparagus serve only as a reminder of the increasing austerity of existence. But now, we could wallow in it, and we did.

Then there were long rows of broad beans, producing such rich crops that they could be picked when they were very young and cooked whole, or better still, podded when they were no larger than peas. There is a subtle emotional pleasure about opening broad beans at this stage, particularly on a hot summer afternoon in an ancient garden. They are so green and tender and innocent; they lie on their white velvety linings like expensively cossetted babies; it seems almost a sin to devour them. This sort of bean has almost vanished from the contemporary scene; most of those which one buys at the greengrocers have such leathery skins that they are only fit to be put through the mincer.

Perhaps the most exciting vegetable in this remarkable garden was one which could not be said to have 'vanished' because—in England at any rate—it has scarcely been discovered. This was described by Oldfield as 'New Zealand spinach', which was how it was known in Victorian days, but if you were to ask for such a thing at even the most exotic greengrocers you would be met by a stare of incomprehension.

'New Zealand spinach' is something of a mystery, but it is a mystery well worth solving. If I were condemned to eating only one vegetable for the rest of my not very natural life, this is the vegetable I should choose. But you will never be able to eat it at all unless you are prepared to grow it from seed, and even then you must know what to ask for, which is . . . take your pick . . .

> Swiss Chard
> Silver Beet
> Sea Kale Beet

Look these up in Mrs Beeton, and you will draw a blank. Look them up in Constance Spry and you will again draw a blank, though Constance has a brief reference—(under spinach)—to 'the wide midriff of a large leaf which may be cooked like spinach or sea kale, and served plain with melted butter or braised.' No other cookery book that I have seen mentions it at all. But do not despair. The excellent firm of Suttons Seeds Ltd sells the seeds under the name of Swiss Chard, with the following legend on the packet . . .

'A leaf beet with no edible root. The midribs and stalks are silvery white and delicious cooked and served like Asparagus or Sea Kale; the foliage is cooked like Spinach. Sow mid-April or May in rows two feet apart. Thin out to one foot apart on soil which has been deeply dug and manured the previous season.'

I apologize for going on about Swiss Chard, but it would be sad if this epicure's delight were to disappear completely from the culinary stage. Cooked by Gaskin it was not only delicious to eat but delicious to look at. Although he cooked it whole, he used to tie back the spinachy leaves before plunging the stalk into boiling salted water. Then, after five minutes, he would allow the leaves to flop down so that they cooked together. When they were tender, he drew them out, shook off the water, folded the leaves neatly round the stalk, and laid them, piping hot, on a silver dish. They were as pretty as Chelsea China and—to coin a phrase—they melted in the mouth.

This, of course, is not Television Cookery, about which I should like to say a brief word.

My chief objection to Television Cookery, as portrayed in the Commercials, is that it seems to be conducted exclusively for the benefit of tiny tots. Whatever may be cooking—baked beans, fish fingers, custards— one may rest assured that the Commercial will end on a close-up of some sticky infant, its chin dribbling with raspberry mousse, or some such concoction. As this terrible spectacle looms closer and closer, there are appropriate sounds, in the background, from Mum and Dad. Mum, gazing at the infant with professionally concealed distaste, assures ten million 'viewers' that the concoction is full of vitamins, and that the infant would perish without it. A quick flash to Dad, in the doorway, licking a dollop of mousse with a pale pink tongue. To make us all feel happier Dad is usually a British workman, hot from the bench or the garage, clad in his working clothes. Perhaps the worst of the food advertisements are those which deal with dairy products. In these the actors, who have seldom strayed far beyond Chelsea, are usually portrayed as farm workers clad in smocks. They speak a strange rustic esperanto of their own invention, and sometimes, to emphasize the bucolic character of the occasion, they slap a cow on the bottom. But always the scene ends with the aforesaid infant greedily devouring a biscuit spread with butter or margarine, while Mum and Dad hover in the background assuring us—to a fusillade of bird music—that it is 'full of country sunshine'.

The 'country flavour' of the cooking at Merry Hall was enhanced by Gaskin's decision to experiment with some of the ancient recipes in *A Receipt Book of Cookery*—the seventeenth-century manuscript volume which I had discovered walled-up in a cupboard at the first cottage I ever owned.* I was attracted to the book not only by the romantic circumstances in which it came into my possession but also by the simple poetry of the language in which the recipes were expressed. Some of them had the sweetness of a lyric by Herrick . . . for example 'To Preserve Quinces Red or White'. That is surely a phrase that should be set to music. Or again . . . 'To Make Slip-coat Chees. The Lady Bray's Recipe.' This evokes a whole social scene, a dance in an echoing barn, with the lady of the manor moving graciously among her tenants.

To Gaskin the appeal of the book was not literary but severely practical. He saw it as a challenge. I suspect that he was sometimes bored by following the familiar recipes, and he was certainly bored by the slick formulas of the glossy magazines. He seldom used strong language but once, surprising him in the kitchen, I saw him throw a copy of *Woman's* something-or-other across the kitchen table with the single contemptuous phrase . . . 'Silly bitch!'

Then, when he saw me . . . 'I beg your pardon, sir, but

* This manuscript has since been published in a limited edition by Cecil and Amelia Woolf under the title of *In an Eighteenth Century Kitchen*, under the editorship of Professor Dennis Rhodes.

some of these women are Too Much of a Good Thing.'
He pointed to the photograph of the glamorous model
who had been chosen to illustrate the recipe. It was for
Toad-in-the-Hole, and she had apparently decided that it
was best prepared in deep evening dress, revealing a very
daring cleavage. 'All lip-stick and nail-varnish, that's
what they are.' He sniffed and threw the paper away
again. '*I'd* give her Toad-in-the-Hole; that's what *she*
needs.'

He did not elaborate the metaphor, and I did not pur-
sue the conversation, which might, however subtly,
have disturbed the delicate balance of our relationship.
We discussed almost everything under the sun, but we
never discussed sex.

Gaskin's first practical experiment with *A Receipt Book
of Cookery* was devoted to the concoction of Cowslip
Wine. It was mid-May, and the old ramshackle orchard
was glistening with cowslips, thronging through the
long grass grouping themselves, joining hands, disper-
sing, reappearing in duets and trios, as though they were
obeying the directions of some shadowy choreographer.
Cowslips are one of my ninety-nine most favourite
flowers. The very word 'cowslip' has infinite echoes of
youth and the days of innocence. And so it was with
mixed emotions that I encountered him one evening,
emerging from the orchard with an armful of these
blossoms, blazing against the lapels of one of his dark-
blue double-breasted suits, which he insisted on wearing,
even for the most rural occasions.

'But Gaskin, I didn't want those to be picked.'

'I shall be needing them, sir.'

'But what for?'

'A little experiment, sir.'

With which I had to be content.

A month later I tasted the results of the experiment in
my first glass of cowslip wine and though it could not
be described as the nectar of the gods, it was very

pleasing, not only for its flavour and its potency—pale amber in colour, with the scent of spring—but for its associations. I sipped it on the lawn, at the end of a tiring day, and the bees soon learned about it, and began to hover around, making soothing noises. Indeed, one of them fell into the jug, and had to be extracted in a bedraggled condition, and gently deposited on the grass.

Here is the recipe:

To Make Couslip Wine Very Good

Take 3 gallans of water put it to 6 lb of lofe sugar boyle it to gather half an hower or beter wn ye scum ariseth take it of & yn power it into a earthen steane scolding-hot to your gallen of picked couslips wn it is most could[13] take a spunfull of yeale est[14] beat it well with 18 sponfuls of serrup of citturn or lemon if it can be got bruing it together with a dish very well well with ye liquear & let them work for to or three days yn strain it forth & wn it have done working over stop it close & in three weks or a month bottle it up puting into every bottle a lump of sugar cork it close.

In spite of the archaic spelling, most of this recipe is easily interpreted. However, it should perhaps be explained that 'most could' means 'almost cold' and 'a spunfull of yeale est' stands for 'a spoonful of yeast'.

Not all the recipes in this book sounded so attractive. 'Miss Leblanc's Receit to Stew Carp', for example, suggests that its author was not a lady of very delicate sensitivity. She begins by telling us to 'take your carps and cut them round ye nape of ye necke to make them bleed; cut up ye belly, take out ye liver and guts, but do not break ye gall, mix ye gravy in ye Stewe Pan with ye blood . . .' Not an alluring procedure. But then, if one takes a long, hard look at the slabs of the average butcher's shop, one must admit that few of the items have much appeal, either to the eye or to the brain.

Gaskin contented himself with more delicate experiments, and like myself he seemed to be attracted by the charming language and spelling in which the recipes had been inscribed. As we turned the pages we walked with 'cabbidges' and 'artichoaks', filling our shopping baskets with 'coucumbers' and 'orringes' and 'apricocks'.

I even tried my own hand at one of the recipes, and I will print it merely because of the music of its prose.

To Candy Flowers

Take gum Arraback & lay it in steep in rose water till it is desolved then take white sugar Candy & bruse it very small then take your flowers in ye heat of ye day and lay them upon ye bottom of a Sive & wet them over wth ye gum water & strow ye sugar candy upon them & set them into ye Sun to dry & as they doe dry put off ye sugar Candy upon them & when ye one side of them is dry & candied then turn them & candey ye other sid of them in ye same manner & so use them as your pleas.

What could be prettier than the idea of such a sweetmeat? It seems to belong in a silver pot-pourri bowl on the table of a Queen Anne rectory. However, the reader should be warned that in fact—as prepared by the author, at any rate—it is exceptionally distasteful, and leaves one with the sort of taste in the mouth which would result from a weekend devoted to licking the backs of envelopes.

CHAPTER 7

Dining with the Rich

MY attempt to introduce a chronological pattern into these reflections must now be abandoned. Except in a mystery story, where the shelves of the larder are linked with the contents of the medicine chest, chronology and cookery have no connection.

So let us forget the unities, say goodbye to Merry Hall, and survey a wider landscape.

I should like to say a word about dining with the rich, not only because it might be practically instructive, but because it might have some interest as a period piece. Most of those people who have dined in houses where money was no object are already dead. Those who survive have lost either their teeth or their memories, and usually both.

This reminds me of my last encounter with Noël Coward, in his villa at Montreux, a few months before his death. As I bent over the bedside to say goodbye he said, with an air of command 'Next time, you will stay a little longer.' I nodded, and looked out through the window, onto a very lovely landscape over which the sun was setting. Then I said something which with the benefit of hindsight, had better been left unsaid. 'If there is a next time. At our time of life one meets people at a party and three weeks later one's reading their obituary notices in *The Times*.'

Crisp and clear, with the authentic timbre of the Master's voice, came the retort. '*I* consider myself lucky if they last through luncheon.'

Which is my last memory of a great genius and a dear friend.

Incidentally, Noël was an atrocious cook. As a man of all talents—or almost all—he could not imagine that there were arts which he would not be able to master. He had an illusion that he could make pastry, and in one of the last interviews he ever gave he boasted of this accomplishment with some complacency. (This interview was privately recorded in a London studio and must be among the rarest items in the vast collection of Coward curiosa.) He spoke of his pastry as though it were as light and delicate as his dialogue; it was, in fact, as flat as a slab of Brecht, as I discovered when I stayed with him during the days when he had a house at St Margaret's Bay. Since everything about Noël has always fascinated me, and always will, I make no excuse for recalling that this was the occasion when he locked me up in his studio. I had been studying his paintings, which were gay and sparkling and full of humour, and I must have betrayed some irritation at the multitude of his talents because he sharply rebuked me. 'Nonsense, Beverley, you have an inferiority complex. Anybody can paint. *You* can paint. What's more, you will paint.' With which he propelled me into the studio, stood me in front of an easel, thrust some brushes into my hand, and strode out of the room, locking the door behind him and announcing that he would return within the hour.

This was a nightmare situation. The minutes ticked by, but no inspiration came. In desperation I decided to do an 'abstract'. After all, any half-witted child can do an 'abstract' and judging from the majority of ultra-modern art exhibitions, a great many of them do. So I squeezed out a tube of gamboge yellow and painted a snake in the top left hand corner. It looked quite pretty, so I painted another snake in the opposite corner, which looked even prettier. The snakes, by an obvious process of reasoning, suggested the Garden of Eden, so I changed over to green and painted the Tree of Knowledge in the centre, with Adam and Eve (in shocking pink) at the base. Oddly enough, both of them looked more like snakes than the real ones, but it was too late to change the design, so I went on painting snakes until he returned.

He marched over to the canvas and surveyed it with his head on one side. Then he said . . . 'Paul Klee. Yes, Beverley, you have painted an authentic Paul Klee. You should call it "Study in Spaghetti".'

I have sometimes wondered whether this episode gave him the inspiration for 'Nude with Violin'.

But at least my picture was better than his pastry.

The richest man with whom I ever dined was William Randolph Hearst. The name of this newspaper Colossus may still ring a bell even with the younger British generation, if only because of *Citizen Kane*, the masterly film which was made about him by Orson Welles. Hearst has sometimes been called the American Lord Northcliffe, but this is a libel on Northcliffe. Hearst was sullied with the dirtiest scum of American politics and internationally he was an ignoramus. Northcliffe, though often misguided, was politically immaculate, and he surveyed the international scene—particularly during the First World War, with the penetrating eye of a prophetic genius. Both men, in their various ways, were mad. But Hearst was mad all the time, with an exceptionally nasty form of superiority complex, whereas Northcliffe only lost his reason in the last tragic months of his explosive life.

Back to the dinner table. The party was in Hearst's ultra-super-colossal apartment in Riverside Drive, New York City. This was the sort of place where you would expect to find a Wurlitzer organ in the lavatory, which would burst into the Hallelujah Chorus as soon as you pulled the plug. The only reason I had been asked was because the editor of one of the Hearst periodicals had suggested that I should write a dainty little piece about the guest of honour, Hearst's mistress, Marion Davies, in which I might helpfully remind the American public that she combined the genius of Sarah Bernhardt with the elegance of Yvonne Printemps and the beauty of Helen of Troy. The piece was never written.

My most vivid memory of Hearst's dinner party was the table decoration which confronted me when I took my seat. It consisted of an entire stag, tastefully arranged athwart the table cloth. The interesting thing about this somewhat bizarre aid to digestion was the fact that I was not even aware of the stag until the end of the first course which, needless to say, was caviar—grey, Beluga caviar, served by the bucketful.

Why, the harassed housewife may ask, were you unaware of so substantial an object? 'In *my* dining-room,' she might protest, 'I could hardly arrange a stuffed stoat on the dining-table, which seats five at a pinch, without arousing comment. How can you expect us to believe that you were faced by an entire stag which escaped your attention until you were half-gorged by your beastly caviar?'

For a number of reasons. To begin with, the stag was partially veiled by quantities of dead pheasants and partridges, still wearing their sad plumage, which had been delicately draped around its hind quarters—(presumably by a bevy of interior decorators)—so that it ceased, in some strange way, to be a stag, and was transformed into a detail which blended into the over-all monstrosity of our surroundings. I use the word 'monstrosity' in its most literal sense, as a symbol of sheer size.

Everything about Hearst was outsize (except, of course, his friend Miss Marion Davies, who became more firmly petite as the years advanced). Look away from the stag, for a moment, and cast your eyes up to the ceiling. It is much further away than you might have expected. Why? Because Hearst, intent upon loftiness—(this does not apply to the moral tone of his newspapers)—had bought the enormous apartment immediately above him and eliminated it. Result, loftiness. Turn in your seat, and look at the distant face of the footman who is serving your caviar. (There is a footman behind every chair.) Again—a sense of loftiness. Hearst had many things in common with Frederick the Great who liked his body-guards to be upstanding—in every sense of the word.

The effect of height is complemented by the effect of length. The table must be one of the longest which was ever put together in one piece, and was probably wrenched—for a consideration of a million dollars—from a Cistercian monastery in Bologna. As a result the guests are seated about six feet apart. This is a discouragement to intimate conversation. As for 'general' conversation, it could only be conducted by a sergeant-major of the Grenadier Guards, equipped with a powerful loudspeaker. The guest on my right is Elsie de Woolf—(the legendary lady who made millions by selling dubious Louis Seize commodes to Chicago meat-packers). Since she is rather deaf, and since in any case neither of us have anything to say to one another, conversation flags. The guest on my left is George Gershwin. One of the ladies had chucked at the last moment, which accounts for the proximity of two males. He doesn't want to talk, anyway, for he is tapping out rhythms with his fork. As for the guests on the other side of the table, what with the stag and the dead pheasants and the be-ribboned antlers,

I could hardly see them at all, let alone carry on any sort of intelligent conversation with them.

All this is long, long ago, over the hills and far away. The Hearst Empire has crumbled; most of his ideals—if they could be called 'ideals'—have been exposed as evil or ridiculous or both; Riverside Drive is no longer the purlieu of millionaires; and the extraordinary clutter of objects which he gathered round him have been scattered to the four corners of the globe. But I thought it was worth recording this little detail of the stag. It is improbable that we shall look upon its like again.

Apart from the caviar I can recall only one item on the menu—terrapin. This was a very rare form of North American turtle which, as I was later informed, was colloquially known as the diamond-backed turtle—a suitable appelation. George Gershwin, leaning towards me and speaking à haute voix, informed me that it cost twenty dollars a portion, which I can well believe, for it was the most delicious thing I have ever tasted. I had never had it before, have never had it since, and doubt whether I shall ever have it again.

One of the nicest things about dining with the rich—by which I mean the *very* rich, the ones with yachts, if they are international, and—if they are British—the ones with so many rolling acres that when they look out of their bedroom windows they have to reach for a telescope to ascertain the extent of their estates—is the fact that they sometimes condescend to take part in the actual preparation of the meals which they serve to their guests.

When I lived in Huntingdonshire, and wrote a book called *Down the Garden Path*,* the local ladies and gentlemen began to call, impelled no doubt by curiosity to find out what sort of person it was who had found so much to laugh about in the little village which, although it was

* Reprinted in *Gift of a Garden*, W. H. Allen, 1971.

on their doorsteps, had never struck them as particularly funny. Among the callers was an old lady by the name of Lady Lilford who lived in a vast and very beautiful mansion which was called, strange as it may seem, Lilford Hall. Since the mansion itself was situated in the village of Lilford there was no great difficulty, when you arrived for luncheon, in finding your way, particularly as Lilford Hall boasted one of the finest private aviaries in Europe, so that the local airs were vibrant with the screams of peacocks, and the squawks and groans and chatterings of innumerable other feathered creatures.

We always inspected the aviaries before luncheon, with Lady Lilford leading the way in an invalid chair, which she propelled with great velocity down the long gravelled paths, like a dowager Stirling Moss, hooting warning signals at distant gamekeepers—hoots which mingled with the aforesaid cacophony of the birds. After this salutary exercise, we returned to the house to partake of a very special sort of sherry which was so ancient and exquisitely distinguished that it tasted of absolutely nothing whatsoever. Having smacked our lips over this spectral fluid, we put down our glasses—longing for a gin and tonic—and drifted into the dining-room.

All the food that was set before us was invariably excellent, but the main feature was always the salad, of which the ingredients stood on the sideboard in various vessels of crystal and silver. When the moment came for its preparation, a footman placed these objects on a tray of Georgian silver, which he bore to the head of the table, in order that the butler might reverently remove them and place them on the table in front of our hostess. The making of the salad dressing then began, and perhaps I was perverse in finding the whole procedure rather funny, but I did, and still do. For one thing it was conducted with such solemnity that it completely stopped conversation. In a deathly hush her ladyship's fingers hovered over the table, squashing hard-boiled eggs with silver spoons, mixing them with French mustard, adding thin trickles of olive oil, pinches of herbs, squeezes of lemon juice, etc., etc., while we watched with almost vulgar curiosity. This was another ritual of a vanished age, and the reason I found it funny was because it really was not very necessary, in view of the fact that the Lilford kitchens commanded the services of a chef, a scullery maid, a tweeny, and a pantry boy.

But it was also, in its odd way, rather touching. This was the old lady's crowning hour. She was a woman of great dignity and intelligence, and in her day she had also been a woman of commanding energy, active in good works, tireless in the conduct of her estates. Now, she was riddled with arthritis, crippled and confined by the humiliating limits of her invalid chair. Nor was her memory quite as sharp as it once had been. But she never forgot to make her salad dressing, which—in her time— she had prepared for no less a person than the Prince of Wales.

I sensed that this dressing might have a sort of symbolic significance for her, so one day I asked her if I might have the recipe, guessing that she might feel pleased at a young man's interest. I had guessed correctly. She was very pleased indeed, and when she had written it down, and handed it to me, she said, 'One day, you must put it in a book.'

Which is what I have done though not, perhaps, in a manner of which she would entirely have approved.

I don't suppose that there is anything so wonderful about this recipe, apart from the lovage, to which she introduced me. A strangely neglected herb which one scarcely if ever finds in the shops, though it is as easy to grow as mustard and cress. It has a very subtle tang of smoked celery.

Apart from the lovage, the housewife will no doubt have all the ingredients ready to hand, with the possible exception of the chef, the scullery maid, the tweeny, the pantry boy, the footman and the butler. For these she should apply to the nearest labour exchange.

LADY LILFORD'S SALAD DRESSING

Herbs. Lovage, tarragon, parsley, chives.

2 hard-boiled eggs
1 tablespoonful tarragon vinegar
1 tablespoonful wine vinegar
1 tablespoonful lemon juice
1 dessertspoonful Worcester sauce
4 tablespoonsful olive oil
6 tablespoonsful single cream
English mustard (made), to taste.

Chop herbs finely, crush egg yolks and mix with herbs. Add oil slowly, then Worcester sauce, vinegar, lemon juice, mustard. Finish by whisking in a bowl.

This will be a very short section, inserted merely to add point to the preceding paragraphs.

I suggested that there was a comic element in the concoction of Lady Lilford's salad. Let me suggest that there is an even more comic element in another of the customs which are invariably followed when one is dining with the very rich—the ceremony of Blowing Out the Candles.

This is worthy of a footnote to the pages of some social historian of the future. I first realized its significance as a very young man, when I spent my first (and last) weekend at a house of overpowering grandeur in the Highlands. We had been entertained at dinner by the sound of bagpipes played by various family retainers, swirling round a lofty dining-room whose walls were draped with the mournful heads of slaughtered stags. We had been dined, and dined very well. The port had 'gone to the right'. (Another footnote for our future social historian.) Cigars had been offered; the bands of the cigars had been removed and crumpled into the ash-trays. (Long ago the British aristocracy decided that any man found smoking a cigar with a band on should be cast, socially, into outer darkness.)

And then, we blew out the candles. Puff, puff . . . and again puff. A strong straight puff from our host, who once commanded the Life Guards. A sly and rather suspect puff from His Excellency. (In those days no weekend party in the Highlands seemed to be complete without some sort of ambassador, even if he had only recently been dragged from a swamp in South America.) Puffs of all varieties. Finally, over the last candle, a thin-lipped judicial puff from Lord Reading—the only member of the party who had occasionally recognized my existence. As he puffed, he caught my eye and smiled.

'A charming ritual, is it not?'

I replied that 'ritual' was precisely the word I should have used, if I'd had the wit to think of it.

'Thank you.' His eyes—the keenest eyes that ever lit the Courts of Law, surveyed the guests, who were beginning to follow their host to the door. 'Whenever I am present on these occasions I am reminded of a group of elderly boy-scouts, among whom I must include myself. We have been dined and wined. We have been waited on, hand and foot. We have not lifted a finger to fend for ourselves. But when dinner is over, we must play our part. We must do our good deed for the day. And so . . . we blow out the candles.'

When I went to bed that night I wrote down those words, which still carry a strange, evocative music. 'Blowing Out the Candles.' They connect socially and harmonically with the historic phrase which was to be used in later years by Lord Grey. 'The lights are going out all over Europe.'

Dining with the rich does not necessarily mean dining well, especially in these days, when so few women have their own cooks. Only too often the dinner is ordered from a catering firm, which provides it at so many pounds a head, together with the people to serve it, who look like—and frequently are—unemployed actors playing the role of butlers and footmen. Even when the hostess *has* a cook the result can be unpredictable. I shall never forget a certain Christmas eve when I attended a dinner party given by an enormously rich woman who was firmly convinced that she was a reincarnation of Marie Antoinette. Since, in appearance, she suggested a small Jewish ferret, the illusion was not shared by her guests; nevertheless it persisted, and encouraged her in her conviction that money can buy everything, including a cook. But a cook is among the few things that money cannot buy, as the occasion was to prove. For this particular cook, a lady who had been imported from darkest Portugal on a film-star's salary, decided to become firmly intoxicated, and drank the bottle of brandy which had been reserved to pour over the Christmas pudding in order that it might be served to the guests in a sheet of expensive flame. As there was no more brandy, she drenched the pudding in Scotch whisky which—for your information—does not catch alight. Time after time she tried to set it on fire, dropping the dead matches at random over the pudding, while it grew slowly cold. In this condition, looking like an obscene and moribund hedgehog, it was hoisted onto a priceless silver platter, and handed round by an equally intoxicated 'butler', who was feeling unusually disgruntled because—if his agent had not been so incompetent—he might at that very moment have been playing the role of one of the Ugly Sisters in a pantomime at Golders Green.

My own reaction to this incident, apart from physical nausea, was one of irritation. If only the rich had any sense they could have as many servants as they wanted, and good ones. It is simply a question of money. The woman who gave her guests this terrible alcoholic hedgehog pudding could well have afforded to pay an expert married couple £100 a week, *and* given them a freehold cottage into the bargain, *and* left them a legacy of £50,000. I refuse to believe that she could not have found people to work for her on these terms. Her only problem would have been the legacy, in case they were nasty people, and decided to poison her. She would have to contrive the legacy so that it would not be payable unless she lived to the age of eighty and then, when she was eighty, alter it so that it would not be payable until she reached the age of ninety, after which she would probably not care very much. Such an arrangement might lead to an occasional strain in domestic relationships, but at least it would assure the elementary comforts of country life.

The eccentricities of the rich, in the matter of entertainment, are most marked in the matter of drink. Take the case of the late 'B' Pembroke—a splendid old lady for whom I had considerable affection. She was in fact the dowager Lady Pembroke, and to be sure that nobody forgot it she issued her weekend invitations on writing-paper headed 'From the Dowager Countess of Pembroke and Montgomery'.

'B' Pembroke, for most of her long and not too tranquil life, had been very frank indeed. For many years she had reigned over Wilton, one of the stateliest homes of England, indeed of Europe. The Pembrokes were part of English history, and she never forgot that she had a Position with a capital P. Once, when I was staying there, she told me of the first dinner party that she had given at Wilton as a young bride. The guest of honour was Kaiser Wilhelm II. He gazed round the vast room; his eyes lingered on the masterpieces that lined the walls.

'Such treasures, Lady Pembroke. Such taste. So many objects of beauty from all over the world. Your family must have been collecting for centuries.'

'I believe so, Sire.'

'But with all these riches have you no fears that one day you might lose them?'

'None at all.'

'And why is that?'

Young Lady Pembroke looked the Emperor straight in the eyes. 'You must remember, Sire, that we have a navy.'

Yes, 'B' had superb quality, and I would not wish to write anything about her that would give pain, either to her distinguished ghost or to her equally distinguished descendants. At the same time, it does seem apposite in this context to mention that 'B', in her old age, used to do very peculiar things with the gin. By which I do not mean to say that she tippled; she was abstemious, and contented herself with a thimble-full of Dubonnet which she sipped before dinner with a slightly apprehensive expression, as though she feared that it might explode.

The gin to which I refer was the gin on the drinks tray—(massive George II silver, exquisitely chased, brought in by the butler at five minutes to eight precisely, to inflame us—but not too violently—before we went in to eat). This gin—purchased at cut prices from some remote wharf in the East End of London—was very cunningly apportioned in the decanter. Mathematically, mysteriously, there were always two fingers of it . . . no more and no less. Two fingers, about an inch and a half, enough for a single dry martini. How was this miracle accomplished? Did Lady Pembroke, half an hour before dinner, when her guests were getting ready or tarting themselves up, creep out of her bedroom and hobble downstairs to empty most of the bottle into a Grecian urn? We shall never know. But the whole thing was so tiresome, particularly for myself, because I was always given the task of mixing the cocktails—that eventually I revolted. 'B' had a very ancient poodle with whom I made friends. It was small, female, scruffy, and almost blind. It used to follow her everywhere, bumping into the furniture and, though it could not be described as handsome, we established an affectionate relationship, and I used to take it for precarious walks in the garden, giving it gentle prods in the right direction and lifting it up when we approached a flight of steps.

One day I came down early to find the poodle waiting for me. There were feeble demonstrations of affection and tottery steps towards the window. The butler came in with the tray. I looked at the poodle and said . . . 'You are bored. So am I. We both need refreshment.' With which I poured a small trickle of gin into its water bowl. The result was instantaneous. After a few laps, the poodle sneezed, shook itself, hiccuped, and walked towards the window. Its progress across the lawn, though erratic, was far brisker than usual, and on approaching the steps it actually managed, after a few more hiccups, to negotiate them unassisted. 'You have quite won Fifi's heart,' said 'B' on our return. Her eyes strayed towards the water bowl. 'I think you both deserve a drink.' So did I. But I thought it wise to change the water in Fifi's bowl before I pointed out that the gin bottle was empty.

I wonder what future generations will think of people like 'B' Pembroke? They are very easy to ridicule—the late ladies of the stately homes. But is the ridicule justified? 'B'—as we noted in her encounter with the Kaiser—had great qualities. She had a shining courage. She would have died for Wilton, and all that it represented; quite literally she would have died, standing on the steps, facing the invading enemy. And when, in the natural course of events, her reign at Wilton came to an end, she stepped aside with quiet dignity. Any criticism one makes of her must really be a criticism of the society that produced her. Inevitably, she was abysmally ignorant of life in the raw. Her knowledge of 'life below stairs' was nil, which is why she could never keep a butler—even from darkest Portugal—for more than a fortnight. And we may suggest, with some assurance, that she could 'not have told Stork from Daz', or whatever it is that those women on television are forever nattering about.

And yet, she had a place in British history—for me, at any rate. In a world that is increasingly dominated by the image of the Common Man it is occasionally refreshing to recall the memory of an uncommon lady.

CHAPTER 8

The End of a Chapter

THE years sped by; Merry Hall, with its lofty rooms and its delicate balustrades, faded into the background; the scene changed and the stage contracted. Once again we found ourselves where we had begun, in a country cottage. Not so 'country' as the cottage in *Down the Garden Path*,* for the expanses of Richmond Park are less rural than the pastures of Huntingdonshire, but rural enough, and at least *safe*. In this day and age, even if one buys a thousand acres in the centre of an Irish bog one may wake up to find oneself surrounded by a complex of pylons and gasometers, with a new airport looming on the horizon. Not so in my present dwelling, which will also, presumably, be my last. Sudbrook Cottage is Crown Property and we lie under the protective shadow of the Queen, who would not stand for such nonsense.

Throughout all these choppings and changings, these uprootings of furniture and transplantings of trees, one

* Reprinted in *Gift of a Garden*, W. H. Allen, 1971.

figure remained fixed and constant, in the person of Gaskin. I had been afraid that by moving from a 'hall' to a cottage he might feel that we were coming down in the world. If he did, he disguised it very well, and met the whole situation in the spirit of Jeeves.

'We shall still have fourteen rooms,' he reminded me, when I suggested that there would not be much space for the furniture. (The cottage was in fact three cottages knocked into one.) 'That should be sufficient for our Important Pieces.'

Somehow I had not considered any of my possessions as Important Pieces, but the idea was good for morale.

'There will be nowhere to hang the blue Venetian chandelier.'

A moment's pause. And then, with quiet respect . . . 'If you'll forgive me for saying so I shall not be sorry for *that*. I had to get onto the steps to dust it. And we are not as young as we were.'

'Do you think the cats will like it?'

'They will settle down, sir. They always do. Which reminds me that I think we shall need three cat doors instead of the usual two.'

'Would you see to it?'

'I have already done so.'

It need hardly be said that the young man who fixed the cat doors was the son of a 'lady from Norwich', whom Gaskin had discovered within a few days of our arrival. The doors were a great success, and the gentle sound of their swinging backwards and forwards as the cats came in out of the garden and the ancient toolshed became part of the quiet symphony of domestic life. History was repeating itself, and the history that repeats itself is the only sort of history for which I have much affection.

Even though our circumstances were spacially and socially 'reduced', Gaskin managed to invest them with a ghostly elegance, through the medium of our neighbours, past and present. A few weeks after our arrival at the cottage I spent the weekend in Wiltshire and on the Sunday afternoon our hostess took us to have tea with the late Duke of St Albans, to whom she was related. The dukes in my life have been so few and far between that I am not qualified to generalize about them, but as soon as I saw this one coming into the room I could not help thinking of the novels of Georgette Heyer. He was the perfect Heyer duke. Parchment white skin, aquiline features, tapering fingers . . . the lot. And incredibly ancient. Which was why, when I was introduced to him, his reaction was surprising.

Scanning me through heavy-lidded eyes—eyes in which, as Madame Heyer would doubtless have noted, one could see the distant gleam of the Crusades—he observed, with some sharpness:

'Beverley Nichols? I thought Beverley Nichols was dead.'

But that was not the point of the story. When he heard where I lived he pricked up his ears.

'Sudbrook Cottage? Is that near Sudbrook Lodge?'

'Yes. I can see it from my bedroom window.'

'In which case you and I might be said to have some slight territorial connection.'

He then told me the story of Nell Gwynn and the baby. It was, of course, Charles II's baby and when she presented it to him he gave her Sudbrook Lodge as a token of his esteem. But Nell wanted more than that; she wanted a title for her baby, and the king obstinately refused to provide one. Maybe he felt that the English countryside was already adequately bespattered with royal bastards. So one day, when he drove down from London to see her, she delayed the usual dalliance, marched him up to the top floor, seized the baby from its cot, held it out of the window, turned it upside down, and announced that unless he immediately made it a duke she would drop it into the courtyard. Whereupon the king, who must have been in a state of some agitation, promptly entitled it the first Duke of St Albans.

One had heard this story before, in various guises, with numerous modifications of locale, and it was interesting to learn from the lips of the 12th Duke that it was in fact authentic, and that it had all happened on one's doorstep, three centuries ago.

The effect of this story on Gaskin, when I recounted it to him, was most satisfactory. We might have come down from a hall to a cottage but in doing so we had managed to connect ourselves—'territorially'—with the shades of one of the most ancient titles in the land.

There were other consolations. As time went by the garden grew apace and the day came when I opened it to the public for various charitable causes. On these occasions Gaskin was in his element. A less dedicated Jeeves would have resented the idea of hundreds of strangers tramping through his domain, and would most likely have spent the afternoon sulking in his sitting-room. Not so Gaskin. He used to attire himself in a double-breasted suit of tropical blue silk, and seat himself at a table behind the garden gate in order to take the public's money. Sometimes he was partnered by the 'lady from Norwich', who rather terrified me because she was so very grand. She always wore a very large Edwardian hat of black open-work straw which cast macabre shadows on her face.

He also assisted me in coping with the cats, who were always in great demand. Unlike some cats they were accustomed to being treated with deference, and they seemed to revel in the adulation of the multitudes. They used to make carefully timed appearances in the porch—pausing a moment for the photographers—and then walk slowly across the lawn, tails erect, towards the bed of cat mint—(*Nepeta labiatae*)—on which they disposed themselves in attitudes of allurement. The only feline problem was presented by 'Five', the eldest cat, who was approaching his twentieth birthday, and lacked the necessary stamina for these exertions. It was Gaskin who hit upon the solution. 'Five' he decided, would remain in the coolness of his sitting-room and, from time to time, when enough tickets had been sold at sixpence extra a head, batches of visitors would be led through the hall, the door would be opened, and they would be admitted to the Presence. And it was indeed a Presence, for throughout the afternoon 'Five', of his own accord, used to sit bolt upright on the circular Victorian table in the centre of the little room, tail carefully curled, front paws strictly at attention, his green eyes scrutinizing his adorers. The only awkward moment occurred when one especially ecstatic lady from New Zealand suddenly produced an ink-pad from her bag, with the intention of persuading 'Five' to press his paw on it in order that he might sign her autograph book. This gesture, though kindly meant, was ill received.

Here is a story so small, so fragile, that you may need a magnifying glass to read it. It was nearly closing time on a sultry afternoon in July. The visitors were thinning out, and the lawns were showing signs of wear. I had retired to my study and flopped into a chair, under the firm impression that I had done enough, for the moment, to support the cause of the Queen's Institute of District Nursing. Then there was the sound of voices in the distance. I tiptoed to the top of the staircase and looked over the banisters.

And there was Gaskin, at the door of his sitting-room, barring the entrance to a very aggressive looking lady who was waving a protesting camera in his face.

'But this is ridiculous,' she was exclaiming. ' "Five" is the one I particularly want to see. I want to take a picture of him.'

'I am sorry, madame.'

'It will only take a moment.'

'I am afraid that it is impossible.'

'But why?'

Gaskin spoke with unmistakeable hauteur. 'It has been a long afternoon, madame. And "Five" ' . . . pause for effect . . . 'is quite exhausted.'

Now a shadow falls across the page.

The summer passed; the visitors departed; the winds grew colder, sweeping through the ancient branches of the copper beech, sending their leaves scurrying across the deserted lawns. And though life, to all outward appearances, went on as usual, there was in fact a subtle change, a slowing down of the rhythm.

Gaskin was growing old. Well, so was I, and so were we all, but Gaskin was growing old too soon, and he was growing old in the wrong way. It was not only a question of pausing on the staircase, as he carried up the breakfast tray, nor of his finding the shopping-basket too heavy as he carried it home across the Common on his return from the shops. There were other changes, which had nothing to do with the weight of years. He began to forget things. There was even a morning when he forgot to feed the cats. He also began to forget the aforesaid 'Important Pieces', so that the dust gathered on the Pannini, and the Sheraton sofa-table was left un-polished. Most disturbing of all, he seemed to be losing interest in his personal appearance. He had always been immaculate; his own clothes had been as carefully pressed as my own; his hair as regularly cut. But now, his trousers began to sag, and his shoes remained unpolished. So did mine.

One night I came home in the small hours of the morning, and found him stretched out on the kitchen floor. There was a faint smell of gas, and after running to him and bending over him, I switched off one of the jets under the burnt-out kettle, thinking as I did so that life was becoming almost too absurdly like a television serial. But this was no case of suicide. His heart beat strong and steady, and after a few moments he opened his eyes and smiled.

'Would you like me to call the doctor, Gaskin?'

'No, sir. There is no need for that.' He struggled to his feet and straightened his tie.

'What happened?'

'I think it is called a black-out, sir.'

'You must see the doctor tomorrow. And of course I'll get my own breakfast.'

'Very well, sir. But I should prefer to lay your tray myself.'

With which he walked slowly, but quite steadily, to the pantry.

Even then, I did not realize that he was hopelessly drunk.

It was incredible. If anybody was qualified to recognize the symptoms of drunkenness in all its stages and manifestations, I was. My whole life, from earliest childhood, had been shadowed by drink. It nurtured the family tree, and twisted its branches into hideous shapes. It had destroyed friendships and brought myself to the brink of murder.*

But somehow, I had never associated Gaskin with drink. Over the years he had hovered in the background with a gay smile and an ice-cold cocktail glass and . . . yes . . . he had liked his little tipple. But on the few times when it seemed that he might be in danger of taking too much, Gaskin had stepped aside and Jeeves had taken over. Even on this occasion, lying prostrate on the kitchen floor, Jeeves took over as soon as Gaskin opened his eyes. His speech was not blurred, his gait was not unsteady.

Later, I was to learn that he had been drinking more and more heavily over a period of several years, but always he had managed to conceal it from me. But no

* As narrated in my autobiography *Father Figure*, Heinemann, 1972.

. . . it was Jeeves who had concealed it, with all the technique and training of the perfect gentleman's gentleman. Looking back on it all, I have a chilling feeling that Gaskin—the country boy from Norwich who came to play so prominent a part on the stage of my small social life, that Gaskin, on that fateful evening, was already dead and that Jeeves was in final control. In its way, this might be regarded as a variation on the theme of Jekyll and Hyde, with one important qualification, for both Gaskin and Jeeves were very charming people. But which, one wonders, was which? And how? And when? And why?

After this, the domestic rhythm quickened, and it was downhill all the way. The doctor diagnosed scirrhosis of the liver. Well, here I was on familiar ground. I had been an expert on scirrhosis of the liver since the age of ten; I knew all its unpleasant physical manifestations, which reach their climax in acute hepatitis, with its yellowing of the skin and its ochre inflammation of the eyes. Jeeves with jaundice . . . it was unthinkable . . . but it had to be thought about. It gives me some consolation to remember that in the closing phases I was able to step, however clumsily, into his shoes, and to give him some of the service which, over so many years, he had given to myself. Even to the point of taking up his breakfast tray.

It never occurred to me to reproach him . . . why should it? He had fallen a victim to what I have come to regard as the 'Nichols Disease', which throughout history has always been—together with war and syphilis—one of the chief destroyers of mankind. Besides, what words could I have found to express my censure? How could the dialogue have been conducted? If I had said to him . . . 'Gaskin, you are drunk' . . . how could he have replied? Such a statement from myself would have been outrageous, even if it were true, even if he were staggering before me, even if he were reeking of drink. (Jeeves never staggered, and Jeeves was always personally immaculate.) No . . . there could be no words of reproach. They would have destroyed, in a few seconds, a most delicate and precious relationship.

Besides, they would have been pointless. He was too far gone.

My last conversation with Gaskin took place on the morning I drove him to hospital. He had eaten his breakfast, dressed himself in a double-breasted blue suit, and tottered downstairs to his sitting-room. He was lying back in his chair, and he looked ghastly. Bright yellow, with those terrible ochre eyes, and very, very old.

But Jeeves was still animating him, and when I entered the room, Jeeves—like a watchful robot—prompted him to rise to his feet, with his customary decorum. When he sat down again, 'Five' climbed onto his lap, and curled up, and began to purr. (Another reflection so shadowy that you may need a magnifying glass to perceive it. How long would 'Five' go on purring? Why had he climbed so slowly into Gaskin's lap? Why was the little room pervaded with this sense of suffocating Antiquity?)

But there was nothing antique about Gaskin's final directions. He stretched out his hand to the table by his side. It was a very yellow hand, shrunken beyond recognition, but it did not tremble. Nor did his voice tremble when he—or was it Jeeves?—began to speak.

'I have been making out a list, sir, in case of emergencies.'

I began to murmur that he should not have troubled himself when he was feeling so poorly, but he paid no attention.

'Beginning with "Five". He was sick this morning, on the rug in my bedroom.'

'You should have told me.'

'It was before breakfast and I thought I should deal with such matters myself.'

'Perhaps he had been eating grass?'

' "Five" does not eat grass before breakfast.'

'So you think he should see the vet?'

'I certainly do, sir. When he sees him, I think you should mention that he is beginning to have difficulty in getting through the cat door.'

In view of 'Five's' spectacular enbonpoint—the result of twenty years of Gaskin's cooking—this was hardly surprising.

He reverted to his list. 'I believe that you know the names of the tradesmen, sir. To save inconvenience I have written their names and telephone numbers on a pad which I have left in the scullery. I have asked them to deliver their accounts by the month instead of by the week.'

'I hope you will be back before the month is out.'

'So do I, sir. But in case I am not, I suggest that you should watch the greengrocer. Otherwise he might take advantage of my absence. His mushrooms are not always reliable.'

A sudden pang assailed me. What need would there be for such a person now? If somebody suddenly arrived at the door with a box of onions and carrots and cabbages and mushrooms I should not have the faintest idea what to do with them.

He must have guessed what I was thinking for he continued . . . 'You will be needing your morning grapefruit, sir. In the drawer of the sink-unit there is a curved knife for removing the pips. And your salads, which you always do yourself. And I think you have watched me preparing a baked potato.'

From anybody else such a remark would have been heavily ironic, but he meant it kindly.

Grapefruits, salads and baked potatoes. The prospect was not inspiring. I would have preferred to be instructed in the art of preparing his cauliflower Polonaise, which melted in the mouth, and looked like a piece of Chelsea china.

'Then there is the telephone, sir. Have you considered that?'

Yes indeed, I told him, I had considered it, and with increasing apprehension. Throughout the greater part of my life Gaskin had been at the receiving end of this devilish instrument, which must surely be counted among the most potent enemies of authorship, and he had perfected an elaborate technique to guard me against its assaults.

'Perhaps the best thing to do would be to have two of the extensions disconnected.'

'Is that possible?'

'Yes, sir. In fact I have already made the necessary arrangements.'

'Thank you. And now you must stop thinking about me and think about yourself. It is time we were on our way.'

He rose to his feet, took 'Five' in his arms, and buried his face in his warm fur. For a terrible moment I thought he was going to cry. But Jeeves was still in control, and his eyes were quite clear as we drove to the hospital. When we arrived a kindly matron recognized me, because I had recently written a series of articles urging better pay and conditions for Britain's nurses. She smiled at Gaskin and said, 'We shall have to give you VIP treatment.' Jeeves graciously inclined his head. But he was totally exhausted and on the verge of collapse. And ten days later he was dead.

It was midnight when they rang up from the hospital to tell me. It was a very cold night, and the cottage was icy. (I had forgotten to stoke up the central heating stove.) When I put down the receiver there seemed to be an unnatural silence and an extraordinary loneliness. I got up and walked to the piano, with the ridiculous notion of playing something—making something up— that would fit the occasion. Thought better of it, closed the lid. Music may be able to soothe the savage breast, but there are times when it only accentuates the agony.

I went to his sitting-room. Again, this feeling of loneliness and emptiness. I walked over to his armchair, and put my hand on it. 'Five' was asleep in front of the electric fire. Slowly he opened his green eyes and looked up at me. We stayed there in silence, looking at one another. A great deal of sentimental nonsense has been written about the psychic perceptions of animals but of one thing I am quite convinced; 'Five', at this moment, knew what had happened. He knew with an extra assurance, a special clarity, for 'Five', too, had only a few days to live.

That night I broke the rule of a life-time and took two sleeping pills. For the average man this would be quite a moderate dose but I am one of those people who are felled like an ox by even half a sleeping pill, and when I woke up I was still only semi-conscious. I knew that something was wrong, very wrong indeed; there was a feeling of ghosts walking abroad; and everything was so cold, so very cold. Never mind. One would feel better after breakfast.

I reached up and pulled the bell-rope that hung above the bed. There was a faint echo from downstairs, but no other response. I pulled again. I was drifting back to sleep. When Gaskin appeared, I should have to tell him to make the coffee stronger.

And then, lying there in this daze, staring at the ceiling, I heard the sound of footsteps below. The creak of the kitchen door, the faint rattle of the breakfast tray. A pause. Then he began to come up the staircase. The familiar patterns of a life-time were repeating themselves —the physical and emotional patterns—the scent of coffee . . . the anticipations of pleasure or alarm which might be arriving with the morning mail.

I struggled up in bed and smoothed out the blankets to make a place for the tray. Very slowly the door drifted open. I had forgotten to shut the windows and the winds of winter were opening it for me.

And now, the door was fully opened, and there was nobody there. And I was awake, widely and most bitterly awake.

The dream was over.

PART TWO

CHAPTER 9

The Ethics of the Paté

WHEN I first saw those chicken livers, glowering at me from under the meat safe, I was utterly revolted. They were so uncompromisingly bloody; they reeked of the slaughter house. Life had not prepared me for this sort of shock. Chicken livers, till this moment, had meant something discovered in pilaffs, nestling on a bed of rice. They went with shining table-cloths and sparkling silver and coarse white wine. And when one stuck a fork into them, and lifted them to the lips, one was pleasantly allured by the spices with which they had been garnished. There was certainly no thought of slaughter houses.

But now, I could think of nothing else. Blood, blood, blood all over the place. Blood running off the plate and dripping into the sink. I lifted the meat safe, stretched out a finger, and prodded one of them. Too disgusting. One felt like Crippen after he had dismembered his wife in that awful cellar. Bits of Mrs Crippen must have been almost indistinguishable from these chicken livers. And yet, one was proposing to fry her, and eat her, or rather, them. One was not a plain cook, one was a plain Crippen, and it was all profoundly depressing.

We are now in the year 1967, which is the year when I really began to cook. Gaskin had been dead for several months, and during the whole of that period I had managed by myself. Well, not quite by myself. From time to time, charming domestic ladies had appeared at the front door to offer their services having heard on the local grape vine that I was now bereft. Doubtless some of them came merely because they wanted the job but there were others, perhaps, who were impelled by curiosity. The thought of a solitary and possibly prosperous bachelor sitting in melancholy isolation with nothing to eat was too much for their maternal instincts. They had to come and lend their helping hands. If their assistance had remained on a manual footing—(the mixing of metaphors is so pleasantly outrageous that we will let it stand) —the ladies might be here to this day. But it was not like that. I had to cope not only with their hands but their voices. They sang. Without a single exception they sang, some of them quite fiercely, stirring things in saucepans, and announcing usually in a dubious contralto, that there was a rainbow round the corner, or something equally sinister. Worst of all was their curiosity. They oozed round the house, peering into every nook and cranny, and when they discovered any sign of feminine occupation they went almost berserk. One day they found a hair pin on the bathroom carpet. From the way they went on you would have thought that it was a phallic symbol, deliberately placed there to give them ideas.

So they departed, one by one, waving their farewells at the front door—sometimes quite affectionately—and left me to my tins.

I have nothing against tins, as we shall be noting in due course. We could live out of tins from the cradle to the grave, sustaining ourselves with the requisite number of calories and vitamins, and our bodies would come to no great harm. The argument against tins, if there is one, is not physical but mental. When you start eating exclusively out of tins and when, as soon as you are hungry, you automatically reach for a tin opener, you eventually develop a tin mind.

This mental metallization is accelerated if you have to do your own shopping in a supermarket. When I entered my first supermarket, shortly after Gaskin's death, I thought it was quite an exciting place. True, I suspected that a number of the women who were buying things must be slightly dotty because of their habit of staring, with glazed eyes, at piles of precisely identical tins, trying to make up their minds which special tin to select. I felt like going up to them and saying 'darlings, don't be silly, the contents of every one of those tins is exactly the same as the others, there are just as many baked beans in this one as in the next one and they all taste equally revolting so what are you fussing about?'

Again, I was excited by the bewildering variety of choice; these were places to which all the ends of the earth had come; Masefield could have written a modern version of *Cargoes* about them. Patés from France, spices from Calcutta, tomatoes from Italy, peaches from California, herrings from Norway, gherkins from Poland. The things from the Communist countries had a special appeal for me. They seemed to throw a chink of light on life behind the Iron Curtain, although I could never rid myself of the feeling that some of them might contain bombs.

For some time I existed with reasonable satisfaction on tins. But gradually the novelty began to wear off and disillusionment set in. The contents of some of the tins proved to be very different from the legends on the labels, particularly with the 'made-up' dishes. One opened the tin expecting to find a delicious steak-and-kidney pudding, only to be confronted by a soggy heap of paste wrapped round a few portions of gristle. And I began to take a great dislike to my fellow-customers. There seemed to be a special breed of Supermarket Women—brash, bustling and brutal, who charged the store like bulldozers in mini-skirts.

One day I rebelled. My shopping had been more than usually frustrating; everything seemed to be in the wrong place; the women were wildly aggressive; and it had taken me about half an hour to get out. (That is the real hell of supermarkets; they are all too easy to enter but they are almost impossible to get out of. There must be some technique enabling one to get out of them easily but I have never mastered it. One stands aside, trying to assess the time element in the various queues clustering at the turnstile. One chooses the shortest queue, and nips briskly into place, behind an apparently amiable old lady whose basket seems to contain nothing but a tin of sardines and a packet of soap powder. One shuffles forward, feeling very clever, and then, when it comes to the old lady's turn, she is revealed as a fiend, for she bends down and produces a second basket containing enough goods to keep her till Christmas.)

When I got home, after arranging the tins in the larder, where they stared at me like rows of glistening robots, I said to myself 'This has got to stop.' I went back to the kitchen and reached up to the shelf where Gaskin had kept his cookery books. I would choose the first book that my fingers touched, I would open it at random, and I would make the first recipe that met my eyes.

The book was the *Constance Spry Cookery Book*, and I opened it at page 25. The pages had gathered the dust, and they were interlarded with some of Gaskin's own recipes, which fluttered to the floor. I would pick them up later. For the moment, I was engrossed in the recipe which fate had sent me.

CHICKEN LIVER PATÉ

With which, now I come to think of it, this book should really have begun.

We must now get back to Crippen, and face up to the moral problems which we have been evading.

They were summed up in those chicken livers. I won't go on about them at too great length, but I don't think we should forget them altogether. They remind us of a fact that most of us conveniently put at the back of our minds—the fact that if we had personally to slaughter the creatures whose bodies sustain us, the vast majority of us would opt for being vegetarians. (At least I hope we would.) And I am reasonably certain that a time will come, however distant that time may be, when future generations will look back on us in horror, appalled by the thought that we devoured the flesh of our fellow creatures. There have been Ice Ages, Stone Ages, Bronze Ages. We have the dubious privilege of living in the Cannibal Age. There is not really so much difference between human and animal cannibalism; there is not much to choose, morally, between the number of legs you stew in a pot.

I was obliged to write this, uncomfortable as it may be, but having written it, what do we do about it? That was the question I asked myself, standing there in the kitchen. Should I make the paté or should I open a tin of tomatoes? (Even tomatoes might have their sensitivities!) If I did not make the paté, would I have advanced to any measurable extent the well-being of the human or animal kingdoms? No. I was only a tiny unit in a teeming community of fifty million meat-eaters. Even if I were to stand up on a platform in the middle of Hyde Park for a thousand years, and shout my head off and crunch lettuces till my teeth dropped out, I could do nothing. The meat-eaters would carry on, anti-crunching, long after I had expired in a mass of decaying vegetable matter.

This, of course, is sheer moral cowardice. If you are a prophet, a pioneer, a selfless saint, you are not deterred by the weight of numbers. Fifty million to one—so what? A bagatelle! Help me back on to my platform, hand me a lettuce, and let me go on crunching into infinity!

But I was not a prophet, nor a pioneer, nor a selfless saint. I was merely a lonely and all-too-rapidly maturing bachelor with an aching desire to sink into a comfortable chair, at a table which somebody else had laid, and eat a paté which somebody else had concocted.

So I made the paté.

But before we leave this awkward subject, let me suggest that there *are* some 'things that we can do about it'. At random . . .

1. We can make a nuisance of ourselves, as individual citizens, when we hear of some exceptionally brutal examples of the abuse of animals. The paté is a case in point. I happened to learn, by chance, of the gruesome processes that lie behind the production of *paté de foie gras*. The wretched geese are stuffed with food until their livers are diseased, and in the meantime a rubber band is tied round their necks to prevent them from vomiting. If mankind can sink lower than that, I should like to know how. When I found this out I began an anti-*paté-de-foie-gras* campaign, which never really got off the ground, because the editors of women's magazines, strange as it may seem, are not eager to publish Christmas supplements filled with pictures of tortured geese trying not to be sick. However, I got in a few pictures, and a few hundred letters of sympathy arrived, and maybe, as a result, a few less geese were tortured.

2. We can increase our subscription to the various societies—the little ones as well as the big ones—who are vigilant in the cause of animal protection. Moral cowardice again—passing the buck—but better than nothing. I belong to so many of these societies that I will not attempt to give a list of them.

3. At the risk of being bores we can demand free-range eggs, we can keep an eye open for the myriad abuses around us—(our Irish neighbours have a pretty squalid record in these respects with their hideous continental traffic in horses). Etc., etc.

4. We can cherish our guilty consciences. We must never be unaware of that guilt. A guilty conscience is a moral asset that should never be lightly thrown away.

Meanwhile, let us admit that we are cannibals, munching and crunching our way through the last quarter of the most lamentable century that has yet stained the Christian calendar.

We will now make our paté.

But first, a word of warning.

If, like myself as I was in those days, you have never cooked meat before, you must be prepared for something very alarming to happen. Almost as soon as you have begun to fry the chicken livers they begin to turn grey. I call it 'alarming' because it is so unexpected. When I first saw this phenomenon I wondered if I had done something wrong, and went into the next room to check the recipe. But I had done nothing wrong, except to forget to turn off the gas, so that when I returned to the stove the chicken livers were bright black and I had to start all over again.

Preparations in order of importance
  8 ounces of chicken livers
  3 ounces of butter
  1 large onion
  1 tea cup full of stoned black olives
  1 liqueur glass of brandy
  1 clove of garlic
  3 bay leaves.

'Seasoning'. This can mean almost anything you care to make it. In my own case it means going to the shelf where I keep the bottled herbs, sniffing them, and mixing them together until they smell exciting, adding them to the paté at the last minute, and hoping for the best.

Now the drama begins. Turn on the gas, put in the sliced onion and the garlic, adding one ounce of the butter, stir till soft. Add the chicken livers and wobble them around in the mixture for three minutes. Sprinkle on the seasoning and the herbs (not forgetting the bay leaves), go on cooking for one more minute. Then turn off the gas, and—while the whole thing is getting cool— slice it and chop it and pound it till it is as smooth as you can make it. Finally, add the olives, toss in the brandy, and stir in the rest of the melted butter.

The masterpiece can now be transferred to the dish you will be eating it from. All that remains to do is to press it into shape, and put it into the refrigerator. Or into the deep freeze, where it will last for months.

In case anybody accuses me of pinching darling Constance Spry's recipe, I must reply that I have done no such thing. The olives are my own invention, and they make the whole difference to the dish. They give it a most intriguing 'gamey' flavour, reminiscent of grouse that has been properly hung.

My initial success with the paté went to my head and I became something of an expert, taking other people's recipes and ringing the changes on them. One of my most ambitious efforts—strongly recommended and not so expensive as might be imagined—is paté of smoked salmon served with avocado pear. This is quite simple to make. Mince enough smoked salmon to fill a tumbler. Then get another tumbler and put in a tablespoonful of chopped fresh parsley, a tablespoonful of grated onion and a tablespoonful of lemon juice. (On no account use dried bottled parsley, which makes the whole thing taste as if it were destined for the linen-cupboard to keep out the moths. Better omit it altogether.) Then cream up four tablespoonsful of butter and—this is vital—one table-spoonful of anchovy paste—and the whole operation is complete, apart from the mixing. I have seen several recipes for making smoked salmon paté but none which include the anchovy paste, which I would like to think is my own invention. If it isn't—and if, as is all too probable—there are dozens of bosomy cookery ladies bending over their sinks and penning deathless prose about this particular concoction, I can only hope that they will not sue me for breach of copyright. Of one thing I feel reasonably assured; nobody else has ever thought of depositing a pale pink smoked salmon paté in the centre of a pale beige avocado pear. For here we stray from the realm of cuisine into the domain of aesthetics, where maybe I am more at home.

There is only one drawback to this recipe, if you should happen to serve it to the ladies. After they have gasped, and licked their dainty lips, and wiped them on their linen napkins, leaving almost indelible stains which will be reflected in the monthly laundry bill, they lean back in their chairs, with a faintly glazed expression, eager for further delights of a similar nature. And while one is scurrying back to the kitchen, swooping up plates and fiddling with trays, and telling the cats that they have already had their tea and that it is not yet time for their supper, one hears in the background the delicate chime of female, maternal voices in this sort of dialogue . . .

'Of course, darling, men are really far better cooks than we are, don't you think?'

'But infinitely, darling. I can't *tell* you what my Simon did with that capon the other night.'

'Yes, dear, you can, and have. But when I think of Roderick's casserole of pigeons . . .'

Or words to that effect. The dialogue is inclined to lose its sparkle when one returns to the dining-room with four plates of processed ham.

The best paté for common consumption by the ladies to whom these words are primarily addressed—the ladies who are obliged to live in Council houses when they long to dwell in palaces—the ladies who have to make do and mend, and wash up and wipe down, when they feel that they ought to be lying on perfumed couches, gently titillated by peacock fans manufactured by negro slaves of startling virility—the best paté, to come down to earth, is . . .

THE JOYCE KIPPER PATÉ

This is more of a mousse than a paté, but it is so delicious, so easy and inexpensive, that it doesn't really matter what one calls it. Perhaps we had better settle for mousse.

Before giving the recipe, I would like to tell a story.

I first tasted it in a lovely old country house that lies within a few minutes' walk of Winston Churchill's old home at Chartwell. My hostess was one of the most romantic musicians of my middle age—Eileen Joyce. Not only was she romantic with her fingers but with her figure, which was more than alluring. The only trouble about it was that sometimes, when she appeared on television, she looked so pretty that people forgot about her melodic line—which was impeccable, particularly in Rachmaninoff—and tended to concentrate on other lines, which had nothing to do with music.

After luncheon we went up to her music room, and it was there that Eileen told me of the shadow that for several years had thwarted her life—a form of neurosis which is not uncommon among musicians. It strikes out of the blue, making it impossible, in the case of pianists, to play the piano—not merely to play it well but to play it at all. In Eileen's case it struck with special ferocity, and for several years she lived in this shadow, making no music and fearing that she would never make music again.

And then as suddenly as it had come, it lifted.

'It was like a tingling in my fingers. I went upstairs to the music room which had been unused for years, though the piano had always been regularly tuned. I drew back the curtains, let in the sunlight, swept away the dust-sheets, opened the lid over the keyboard, sat down, lifted my hands, waited . . .

'And then it all came back, in a flood, in the form of Schumann's *Carnival*. I struck the opening chords, and I knew that I was going to play it well . . . as well as I had ever played it when there were thousands of people listening to me out there in the darkness of the concert hall. Even when I came to the section of the Paganini variations, which isn't exactly a beginner's piece, I knew that I should sail through it, without a false note. And I did.'

What has all this to do with kippers? Nothing at all, but I make no excuse for telling the story. The sense of hearing and the sense of taste are both powerfully evocative, and when the two are combined, there is magic in the air. Anyway, whenever I hear Schumann's *Carnival* I taste kippers.

Kipper Mousse

Take 4 kippers and poach them in boiling water for 5 minutes.

Set aside a $\frac{1}{4}$ pint of the liquid and dissolve 2 teaspoonsful of gelatine in it.

Bone the kippers, and leave them to cool.

Put them in the electric blender, add the cooled gelatine and a generous pinch of cayenne pepper.

Press the button and while the mixture is whirling round, pour in 5 ounces of double cream.

After 60 seconds stop the blender, pour out the mixture, and leave it to set.

As this is a pleasantly proletarian concoction I serve it from a coarse terracotta bowl set on a straw mat, accompanied by thick slices of toasted whole-meal bread.

CHAPTER 10

A Frenchman comes to Dinner

RENÉ'S restless eyes roamed the kitchen.

'What are you looking for?'

'A cocotte,' he retorted brusquely. 'I cannot see a single cocotte in the kitchen.'

Nor could I; nor, to be frank, did I greatly desire to do so. The only lady who spends much time in my kitchen is my daily, Mrs Chapman, who would resent such an appellation.

'I despair of you, mon cher. A kitchen that does not contain a cocotte! What does one do in it?'

It would have seemed more apposite to enquire what one did in a kitchen that *did* contain a cocotte.

We will elucidate.

René is my French translator. In his case the word is inadequate, for he is a distinguished man of letters in his own right, and when he 'translates' an English work he gives it a special sparkle.

He is middle-aged, electrically vivacious and Parisian. He had come over to discuss my French affairs, and before his arrival he had written: 'We may bore ourselves with business, so I will prepare for you in the space of one hour a ratatouille that will make your mouth water. You will please have ready for me . . .

2 Aubergines
2 Green Peppers
2 or 3 Small Marrows
1 lb Tomatoes
3 Onions
Garlic. (Fresh cloves, if you please, not synthetic.)
Lauro, Thyme. And the usual flavourings.
Olive Oil.'

So here we were in the kitchen, with all these ingredients waiting to be transformed into a culinary delight, talking about cocottes, and before we go any further, I will clear up this ridiculous verbal confusion.

The word 'cocotte', to me, signifies a lady of easy virtue, of the social and moral status of La Belle Otero, and I imagine that it bears this meaning to anybody of moderate sophistication. It is as firmly established in the English language as the word courtesan. (Which makes it all the more puzzling that it is not included in the larger Oxford Dictionary.) However, in France it also means a casserole dish, but a casserole dish with a difference, because it has to have a *lid* which will hold water. René eventually discovered the casserole dish, and for the lid he substituted a deep plate into which he poured hot water. Why this should make so much difference I have no idea, but it did, judging from the ratatouille which he eventually created.

Before we can describe the making of this dish I should explain that during its production we were partaking of a meal that I had prepared myself, beginning with shrimps mayonnaise. Until René's visit I had always entertained the illusion that my shrimps mayonnaise were quite good. They were certainly very easy to do.

One bought a package of shrimps for £1, unfroze it, divided the shrimps into four portions, arranged them in glasses, put them in the frigidaire, and left them there till the guests arrived.

Then—making some cunning excuse about having to feed the cats—one glided out into the kitchen, put a wallop of mayonnaise on top of the shrimps, and transported them to the dining-room. Where they remained until we went in to dinner, when they were greeted by suitable exclamations of delight.

Sometimes, if one wished to enhance the general impression of haute cuisine, one added a touch of garlic to the mayonnaise, and stuck a quarter of a lemon on the side of the plate. This was extremely effective with the ladies, particularly if—(as I now suspect)—they had powerful digestive functions. 'Delicious' they would murmur, champing their jaws. Then they would add that men did things much better, didn't they? And that I must give them the recipe.

This reaction had encouraged me in the aforesaid illusion about the excellence of the shrimps. The only trouble was that I became inclined to overdo it. I would say to Cyril . . . 'Jane and Penelope are coming to dinner on Friday.'

'What are you giving them?'

'I thought we might begin with shrimps.'

'We began with shrimps last time.'

'So what?'

'And the time before. If you go on beginning with shrimps these girls may get suspicious.'

'Of what?'

There is a regrettably coarse strain in Cyril's nature, so we need not record his reply.

We sat down to confront our shrimps, and from the moment I saw them, gleaming in their glasses with their dollops of mayonnaise on top, I felt that something was wrong. The spell was not working. They seemed to have 'suffered a sea change'—no, that is precisely the opposite of what I mean. They seemed to have suffered a *non* sea change; the sea was far, far away, and the deep freeze was casting its shadow over us.

'This wine,' observed René politely, 'is admirable.'

It was. Though how he should have known the name of the château and the precise year was beyond me. Something, I suppose, with merely being French.

The moment of truth had arrived. One of several moments that were to ensue.

'Do you think,' I asked, 'that this wine goes with these shrimps?'

He prodded the shrimps with his fork. I looked into his crinkled, humorous, affectionate, mocking face—the face that I had known over so many years, in good times and in bad—and awaited his answer.

'I do not think, mon cher, that *any* wine would go with these shrimps.'

He was right, of course. Later, he was to explain where I had gone wrong. And maybe, one day, I will try to write something sensible about shrimps. (Though it is difficult to be 'sensible' about them, when one recalls certain evenings in the South Seas, when the flavour of them comes with the cool of the sea-breeze, and the rustle of the palm trees overhead, and the tingle of the sand on bare feet, and all kinds of sensory and extra-sensory perceptions that drift down the years.)

Anyway, I shall never serve shrimps for dinner again. Not in that way.

A nos moutons. To our ratatouille which has been cooking for the past half hour. In order that we may study it from its inception we must set back the clock.

As soon as a Frenchman enters a kitchen the tempo accelerates, and it was only a few seconds before Cyril found himself peeling the white pithy inside from under the skin of the peppers. 'No, mon cher Cyril, your knife is not sharp enough.' Seizing the knife, he searched the drawer. 'It is not to be believed. There are no sharp knives. Ah—here is one.' Cyril began again.

René turned on the gas, seized the cocotte, and tossed in the olive oil. To me, he observed, 'The cocotte, mon cher Beverley, is a word you must not forget.' (I was not likely to do so.) 'C'est l'utensile de base de tout ménage. The basic utensil of every household. Forgive me; I did not remember that you spoke excellent French. Where are the marrows? I must slice them. I want them to make some water.'

For the next few moments his hands flickered over the cocotte, like the hands of a magician, cutting the aubergines and adding them one by one, then the tomatoes and the onions, which he sliced so swiftly that they seemed to fall to pieces in his fingers.

'I seem to be doing nothing but watch.'

'That is the best thing you can do. That is how I learned to cook, by watching.'

My eyes strayed to the sideboard, where there was a large pannier of extra vegetables that I had bought in case he might need them. There was celery, there were mushrooms, and a beautiful bunch of young carrots. Would all these things have to be wasted? After all, ratatouille was a purely vegetable dish, and didn't all vegetables 'go' together?

Greatly daring, I said to him:

B.N. René, what about those carrots?

R.B. Eh bien—what about them?

B.N. Couldn't we use them?

R.B. You should be sent to Siberia. Ratatouille is a plat that is entirely Provençale. And carrots do not grow in Provence.

This, of course, was a lunatic statement. Carrots grow in Provence like mad. (Or do they? Surely they *must* grow in Provence?) However, I did not contradict him.

B.N. And these mushrooms?

R.B. (outraged). You suggest that we put mushrooms?

Do you know what they would do? They would give the smell of the tiger!

(I have not the faintest idea what he meant, but I report the remark in case any real cook can interpret it.)

After being accused of these tigrous intentions I thought it best to omit any reference to the celery.

René had almost finished. 'It will not be perfect,' he said. 'I have been working under a disadvantage. For example, tout l'épluchage doit être faite en avance. You do not know that word—épluchage? It means peeling. Everything should have peeled and prepared. And you should have washed the aubergines. In France one has a horror of pesticides. Never mind. Let me have the salt.'

I handed it to him.

'What is this?'

'Salt.'

'You have no *sea* salt?'

'I'm afraid not.'

Silence, and a deep sigh. Then he shrugged his shoulders, added a pinch of my regrettable substitute, put a plate on top of the cocotte, filled the plate with water, adjusted the gas, and washed his hands. 'We will leave it there,' he observed, 'pour la-laisser mitonner. And since your French seems to be not so good as I had imagined, the word "mitonner" means to simmer.'

I turned to lead him back to the dining-room.

'But, no . . . mon cher Beverley. We have twenty minutes to wait, and there would be nothing for us to do in the dining-room except to sit at the table regarding dead shrimps. This would be disagreeable. We will go into the garden.'

This suited me very well. My morale was sadly in need of a boost. My attempts at cuisine had been disastrous; my knowledge of the French language was obviously almost nil; at least I knew how to make a garden.

But a final humiliation was to come.

On our way out I paused to open the bread-bin, from which I extracted a slice of brown bread.

'What are you doing?'

'I thought we might feed the gold-fish.'

'You feed the gold-fish on brown bread?'

'They like it better than white.'

'But why do you feed the gold-fish on bread at all, when you have such a beautiful melon?' He pointed to a honeydew melon from which a slice had already been cut.

This, I thought, was carrying haute cuisine almost too far. I was beginning to be bored with cuisine, haute or not so haute.

'You mean to say that you feed gold-fish on melon?'

'Not the fruit, naturally. But the seeds.' He took a large spoon and scooped the seeds on to a plate. 'Come, I will show you.'

We walked across the lawn in silence. The garden was almost veiled in dusk; the air was very still; there was a crescent moon and a sprinkling of stars. 'Haute cuisine,' I thought again, wondering if the ratatouille would have begun to scorch. But when we reached the pool it was so beautiful that I forgot all else. It was a dark mirror on which the lilies were sleeping, framed with leaves that were flecked with silver.

René held out his hand and tossed the seeds onto the surface of the water. Whereupon, of a sudden, the mirror came to life. From under the leaves there was a gleaming and a gliding—a twisting and turning of gold and silver fishes that had been roused from sleep by a strange excitement. He threw in another handful of seeds that speckled the water and now, into the silence there crept a curious music, as the fishes leapt to the surface—a tiny staccato symphony to accompany the mystery of the ballet that they were weaving. Plink, plink, plink . . . plonk, plonk, plonk . . . delicate pianissimo sounds so subtle that they could not be transcribed on any instruments that any man has ever fashioned . . . sounds of sheer poetry, coming, so it seemed to me, from waters of great deepness and echoing to skies of infinite height. Plink, plink, plink . . . plonk, plonk, plonk . . . a crowd of gold-fish in a lily pond . . . on a moonlit night of summer.

If haute cuisine contained many such magical moments it should indeed be regarded as a fine art.

'It is time, I think, for you to taste the cognac that I have brought for you. And to tell me what you think of it.'

We have come in from the garden. We have returned to the dining-room, and devoured our ratatouille, which was a poem in itself. We have also comforted ourselves with a Stilton cheese, concerning which, for once in a way, René had no adverse comments. He even asked for a second slice.

I had also placated him with a cigar. A swift comment on this detail. I loathe cigars, and anyway I resent the price one would have to pay for them. The only cigars you will ever find in my house have been filched from such functions as Lord Mayors' banquets. Is this immoral? I do not think so. One has been dined and wined —probably at one's own expense, as a ratepayer—and then a man in livery breathes down the back of one's neck and thrusts a glittering box of cigars under one's nose. What does one do? My own reaction is to appropriate one, and if possible two of these opulent objects, lay them by the side of my plate, and at a convenient moment, when nobody is looking, thrust them into my breast-pocket, hoping that they will not get squashed. It was a cigar of this nature that I offered to René, and judging from his expression of approval as he savoured it, the function from which it had been filched must have been quite an important one.

'Time to taste the cognac.' Splendid. And to tell him what I thought of it. Not quite so splendid. For the cognac was obviously going to be something very special. The bottle had a hand-written label announcing that it was Grande Fine Champagne 1952, and from various hints that René had dropped I gathered that it had emerged from the château of an elderly marquise of almost unbearable distinction, who never gave a bottle to anybody who was not of the blood royal, and even then, only under protest.

I fetched three glasses and placed them before us. This action prompted a very strange question.

'But, mon cher, where are your bowels?'

'I beg your pardon?'

He gestured towards the glasses. '*Have* you no bowels?'

I was at a loss. I had always assumed that I was normally equipped in that respect.

'Vos ballons!' cried René. 'Où sont vos ballons?'

I got it. 'Bowels' meant 'bowls', which in its turn meant balloon-glasses.

'I'm terribly sorry, René. I don't believe we have . . .' I tried to pronounce a word which was a tactful compromise between bowels and bowls . . . 'any bwouls.'

He raised his eyes to the ceiling. 'This friend of mine . . . I bring him a cognac that is a masterpiece and he tells me that he has no bowels.' He shook his head sadly. 'Never mind. We will use these objects, which seem to have been specially designed for Coca-Cola.'

He poured out the cognac. 'And remember, my friend, that one drinks it through the nose.'

As I sipped it I saw what he meant. It was so delicate that it seemed to float through the nostrils, and drift around the palate like an incantation.

'You are drinking it through the nose?' he demanded suspiciously.

'Yes, René.' To reassure him I gave a loud sniff.

He held up a warning finger. 'The nose is not a vacuum-cleaner. Like this.' He sniffed very delicately and gave a sigh of pleasure. And then, in tones of great solemnity . . . 'You must also *chew* it, and *waltz* it in your mouth. You understand?'

No, I did not. But the cognac was so exhilarating that I managed quite a good chewing-waltzing expression, which evidently satisfied him, for he nodded approval. 'All the same,' he sighed, when we had put down our glasses, 'you would have enjoyed it even more if you had some bowels.'

But the cognac, marvellous as it was, could not compare with the miracle that followed.

René went over to the side-board and removed the silver wrapping from one of the presents that he had brought for me in his travelling bag. There was revealed a small bottle—about the size of a half pint—which he placed in the centre of the table. It contained a liqueur the colour of dark rubies and it bore a hand-written label,

Pour
Beverley Nichols
avec les compliments de
M et Mme Carroixe
'Cassis'
Roinville 1966

'Some glasses, please.'

This was a welcome word; it indicated that for the moment, at any rate, the absence of bowels was being excused.

Very gently, very steadily—almost drop by drop—he poured into the glasses the equivalent of a tablespoonful of this mysterious fluid.

'Je ne suis pas avare,' he murmured, replacing the cork, 'but when you drink it you will see why I have been so discreet.' He handed us our glasses. 'And when we drink, if you please, we will drink in silence.'

It will be difficult to describe the next few moments in prose that does not sound as though it had been written by an advertising agent. Perhaps that is being over-scrupulous for, after all, this astonishing creation is not on the market. Even so, though our conscience may be clean in that respect, let me suggest that it will be equally difficult to record in prose that does not sound as if it came from the pen of a suburban and more than faintly intoxicated Keats.

For upon my word, this held the liquid magic of the nightingale. As soon as it touched the lips one's mind resounded with echoes of the immortal Ode. 'That I might drink and leave the world unseen, and with thee fade away into the forest dim.' This admittedly would have been impractical, as the dining-room looked out onto Ham Common, but the memory came inevitably and with it a whole troupe of other memories, cliché joining hands with cliché. 'Cool'd a long age in the deep-delved earth.' Impractical again, because it was only five years old and it was made out of black currants, who resent 'deep-delving'. Never mind. Keats was in the room, at that moment, a pale figure hovering over our glasses, reaching out a spectral hand. I could hear his voice, feel his presence; I could see him writing the first line of the second stanza . . . 'O for a draught of vint-age . . .'

The reader may decide which has won—the publicity agent or the suburban Keats. The general public may be more interested in the actual recipe.

Black Currant Liqueur

Pick black currants at their ripest.

Remove stalks.

Put them in a *glass* jar with half their weight of castor sugar.

Leave for a fortnight, exposed if possible to full sun-light. If sunlight is inadequate leave for three weeks. During this period shake jar every day to ensure that contents are properly mixed.

Filter the liquid through a 'Chinois' and mix with the same amount of alcohol at 90°.

Let it remain for three months, still exposed to sunlight, and then age for four years in bottles.

This recipe, perhaps, needs two comments to make it fool-proof. When I asked René what sort of glass jar was needed, he replied—'Naturally, a bonbonne.' I sought further enlightenment because I did not know what a 'bonbonne' meant; it sounded like two French nannies stuck together. Then he said that it only meant a glass bottle with a big bottom and a narrow top—something rather like Diana Dors. 'Par exemple, a big flask of Chianti.'

The other comment concerns the word 'Chinois'. This is really only a finely meshed sieve. The reason it is called a 'Chinois' is because if you turn it upside down it looks like a Chinese hat.

To be serious for a moment.

I learned a great deal from René on this occasion, and though it would be ridiculous to generalize from so fleeting an experience, I will hastily tabulate the lessons. (The notes that one scribbles on one's cuff are sometimes more valuable than the records that one transcribes in a ledger.)

The difference between French cooking and English cooking . . . no, we will cross that out and start again, for the French no longer hold a monopoly of the art. Nowadays, you can eat as well in England as in France; and, if you know where to go, you can probably eat best of all in America. The most exquisite food that I have ever tasted was in New Orleans, and after that, in San Francisco. Even so, it remains true as a general rule that the highest standard of cooking is to be found in France, just as the highest standard of music is to be found in the Germanic countries. You would have to search very hard to find a French village where you could not get a perfect omelette. And even in the smallest provincial towns of Germany and Austria there is always music in the air—good music, too. I shall never forget a Viennese occasion when I found myself bouncing up and down on a merry-go-round in the Prater. The lights were as harsh as at any English fair, and the shouts of the merry-makers were as hoarse and strident. But the music which accompanied this crazy carnival, even though it blared through the mouths of mechanical trumpets, had been written by Mozart.

So—let us forget our French accents, if we have any, and suggest that the differences between good cooking and bad cooking are as follows.

1. You must be serious about it. A dinner is not a joke; it is an occasion.
2. You must be prepared for it. An artist cannot paint a picture without a fully equipped paint-box. It was only after René's visit that I realized that my own kitchen was lacking in a number of essentials, of which the cocotte was the most obvious example, and I made haste to remedy this state of affairs.
3. You must stick to the rules, by which I mean you must abide by the recipes. If the recipe tells you to use a teaspoonful of something or other you must not use a tablespoonful. One of the surest signs of a bad cook is a tendency to over-improvise, though a certain amount of improvisation is sometimes unavoidable. I have seen women run their hands over the bottles on the herb shelf as though they were running their fingers over the keys of a piano, choosing herbs almost at random. Basil, thyme, tarragon, sage, mace, parsley, any old thing . . . into the pot they go, with the result that the end product tastes of nothing at all. René Brest was right to reprove me for the suggestion that carrots should be added to his ratatouille; this is a dish that the French have perfected over the cen-

turies and it is foolish to imagine that we can improve upon it.

This does not imply that we should never compose our own variations on basic recipes—indeed, doing so is half the fun of cooking—but we should never lose sight of the original recipe, and we should be very certain of the excellence of the variation before trying it out on our friends.

4. Time. Constance Spry once said that 'a good cook is economical in everything but time'. This is certainly true. And while we are on the subject of time, perhaps it is worth observing that this is an element that should be remembered not only by the cook but by her guests. In France—the true France as opposed to the international France of Americanized Paris—dinner at 8 means dinner at 8 and not at a quarter past 8. In our own country it is coming to mean almost anything that the guests care to make.

The Americans are the worst offenders in this respect, and the richer they are the more deplorable their culinary customs. They acquire French chefs and pay them fabulous salaries; they give these chefs a free hand; and then they ask an assortment of their millionaire acquaintances to dinner at 8 o'clock.

What happens?

At 8.45 precisely, the first guest arrives, swathed in mink and over-laden with orchids, to be informed by the Portuguese butler that her hostess is still in the bath but will be down in a moment. This information fills her with such rage and anguish—(she had intended to 'make an entrance')—that she feels like storming out of the house and walking round the block for the next half hour. But alas it is too late, for her mink has already been snatched from her by the Yogoslavian parlour-maid, who has waltzed away with it to hang it up in the neo-Palladian cloakroom.

And now, the bell rings again. 8.50 p.m. 9 p.m. (By now the hostess, very décolletée and reeking of 'Femme', or some such scent, has got out of her bath and come downstairs and is propped up against the fireplace, receiving her guests with an expression of faintly glazed distaste.) 9.10. The last bells are ringing, and the Greek under-footman is already slightly high. 9.20. In comes the guest of honour, aged eighty, who is the President of her husband's Corporation—and, incidentally, is longing to be back in his own bed, with a copy of *The Reader's Digest*, a glass of ice-water, and three digestive biscuits.

This is by no means an exaggerated description of some American dinner parties that I have attended, though it would be unfair to suggest that it applies all over the United States. It would be equally unfair to deny that one has never experienced similar frustrations in London or Paris. The question is . . . how does one deal with the problem, particularly if one is the host? My own solution, which one day I hope to have the courage to adopt, is to begin dinner at the time for which the guests were invited, even if one has to eat alone. And if one can eat it fast enough, to rush out of the house, slam the front door, and leave the offenders ringing the bell without an answer, preferably in a heavy downpour of rain.

Cookery and Sex

NOWADAYS it seems to be almost impossible to sell any commercial product without invoking sex. All the great exhibitions—cars, yachts, washing-machines—are so cluttered up with blondes that one can scarcely see what one has come to buy. They sprawl on the bonnets, loll on the decks and drape themselves round the washing-machines in attitudes which are intended to be alluring, but which to some of us are merely distracting. The blondes have even found their way into the catalogues of the seedsmen, who cannot print a plain picture of an herbaceous border without sticking a blonde in the middle of the hollyhocks.

There is only one department of our lives in which this rule does not seem as yet to apply, and that is in the kitchen. True, there is one deservedly popular television commercial which has constantly assured us that X, a form of meat extract, 'gives a meal man appeal', but it is presented with such discretion, and the camera switches so swiftly from sex to soup, that only a pedant could complain that it was in any way inflammatory. Apart from this, the food industry seems to have by-passed sex, and the cookery-writers might never even have heard of it. If you had mentioned sex to Mrs Beeton she would have thrown the stock-pot at you.

This is a curious omission, and though I should be the last to wish to increase the national quota of commercial blondes, I think that it should be rectified. After all, the three primary impulses of life are fear, hunger, and sex. Fear comes first, for it involves self-preservation. With fear, hunger walks hand-in-hand. Only when fear and hunger are out of the way do we arrive at sex.

So let us discuss sex and cookery, and let us begin in the crudest way, with aphrodisiacs. In case this book falls into the hands of the very junior classes, we will mention that the word derives from Aphrodite, the Grecian goddess of love, and signifies any drug that is calculated to stimulate desire.

By a curious chance, I happen to know quite a lot about aphrodisiacs. I acquired this knowledge in India during the war, travelling by train from Bombay to Calcutta.

The circumstances were bizarre. My companion on the long, sweltering, five-day journey was an American commercial traveller, representing one of the biggest pharmaceutical concerns in the world. He was not an attractive character—purple in the face, and soggy in the paunch, but he held a morbid interest because he was a fanatic, and all fanatics, in their way, are fascinating. His name was Perkins.

Before the train had lumbered out of the squalid suburbs of Bombay, Mr Perkins had introduced himself, clambered up to the luggage rack, and dragged down a heavy suit-case, stuffed with samples of his products. These revealed themselves in the shape of brightly coloured pills, bottles, tubes and jars, whose contents, he assured me, were guaranteed to stimulate the most jaded debauchee.

The conversation went something like this.

'You would be surprised, Mr Nichols, at the enormous consumption of aphrodisiacs in this vast sub-continent. And do you know my theory about it? My *poisonal* theory? My *poisonal* theory is that it is due to the institootion of child-marriage.'

'Indeed?'

'Yes, *sir*. They start too young. You would be surprised, Mr Nichols, at the age when they start.'

'Yes,' I said. 'I'm sure I would.'

'They start so young that they are worn out before they are twenty. Impotent, Mr Nichols. You would be surprised by the amount of impotence in this vast sub-continent.'

·'Quite.'

'They have hardly reached the age of manhood before their powers are sapped. Speaking as man to man, Mr Nichols, their vital parts are *shrivelled*. There is no other word for it.'

Speaking as man to man, I longed to enquire how one unshrivels the vital parts, but it was a difficult question to put into words. So I asked if they were very expensive.

'Expensive, Mr Nichols? Some of them are enormously expensive. You see this bottle here? That is for the Maharajah of X. Aged twenty-two, fabulously wealthy, but *shrivelled*, Mr Nichols. There is no other word for it. You would be surprised if I were to tell you how much he will be paying me for this bottle. You would be even more surprised if I were to tell you what has gone into it.'

I suspected that a great many very disagreeable things had gone into it, so I tried to steer the conversation towards less dangerous topics. Presumably, I said, he did not deal exclusively in aphrodisiacs? He concurred, though with no great interest. I persisted, suggesting that perhaps he also had some nice tooth-pastes, or some refreshing gargles? Oh, yes, he said, he had these things.

But they obviously bored him; he had a one-track mind. As the whole subject was also beginning to bore myself, I took refuge behind the *Times of India*.

But even the *Times of India* did not save me, as the long torrid journey prolonged itself, from further discourses on aphrodisiacs, and by the time we reached Calcutta I could have given a lecture on the subject. As I had suspected, a great many disagreeable things went into them —so disagreeable, indeed so revolting, that the very word still gives me a faint frisson of disgust.

So why bring up the subject at all, in a 'cookery book'?

For the simple reason that the kitchen knows no boundaries, and that its products involve all the human passions. If you question these contentions, stick to Mrs Beeton.

Some twenty years ago Mr Graham Greene gave the stamp of his approval to a book of aphrodisiac recipes called *Venus in the Kitchen*. The sub-title was 'Love's Cookery Book', and facing the title-page there was a painting of exceptional hideousness by D. H. Lawrence, showing a naked woman, bloated and deformed, stoking a stove. It was not only a repulsive little volume but a tragic one, for the author was Norman Douglas, who once wrote a masterpiece called *South Wind*. He was in his eighties, living in penurious and disreputable exile, when he clipped these embarrassing pages together. And though it would have been better if the book had never been published, we may hope that he made a little money out of it. Genius in decay must arouse our sympathy. What is difficult to understand is Mr Graham Greene's enthusiasm. He tells us that this will always be 'one of his favourite Douglas's'. One wonders why.

Venus in the Kitchen is not only a senile compilation— filled with sly hints and feeble attempts at lechery—it is also a fake. Douglas was something of a scholar, and searches his failing memory for aphrodisiac references in classical literature, reminding us that Aristotle recommends the brains of sparrows mixed with the brains of 'pigeons that have not yet begun to fly'. He makes terrible little jokes about Artichokes Bottoms and Pie of Bulls Testicles. 'For persons of cold temperament' he invents fantastic concoctions such as 'Marmalade of Carnations', and tonic wines—warmly recommended by aged friends. It is all very, very sad. Maybe it would not have been worth mentioning the book at all, were it not for the fact that the lustre of Mr Graham Greene's name might persuade some misguided person to buy it second-hand. If he does, his admiration for Douglas as a novelist, and Greene as a critic, will scarcely be enhanced. If he tries any of the recipes, he will merely be sick.

For the very plain truth of the matter is that there never have been, and never will be, anything remotely resembling the legendary love potions of the past. Poor old Douglas does his best to persuade us that oysters inflame the passions, particularly the passions of young gentlemen. I have it on the highest Harley Street authority that they do nothing of the sort. If a young lady, lacking a conventional love potion, were to spend half a week's salary on two dozen Whitstables, to be served on a low table in front of a seductive fire of electric logs —if such a contraption can be termed seductive—she would be wasting her money. The young gentleman would not be inflamed. On the contrary, he would be filled with the gloomiest apprehensions, which would increase with every gulp. He would decide that if this was the style in which his intended proposed to spend her housekeeping allowance, the sooner he changed his intentions the better.

It is the same with stout, which—if imbibed in sufficient quantities—is conventionally supposed to dilate the nostrils, to agitate the organs, and to bring a devilish sparkle into the eyes. It does none of these things. Admittedly, if it is mixed with an equal quantity of champagne, in the shape of 'Black Velvet', and if it is absorbed in a reclining position on a yacht at eleven o'clock in the morning, to the sweet murmur of syren voices, preferably on the Mediterranean, inflammatory symptoms may be encouraged. So may sunburn and indigestion.

As we have observed before, neither the love potions of antiquity nor the 'aphrodisiacs' of today, have any factual basis. All there have ever been, and all that are currently available, are contained in a small selection of highly specialized and extremely dangerous drugs which can still be purchased—by those who are sufficiently besotted—in the shadier purlieus of Port Said and Soho. But no prudent girl, if she knew what went into them, would dream of popping them into the soup.

And yet food and love are so interlinked that it is difficult to think of one without the other. This elemental rule is not always observed by young couples when they dine together. An obvious example is the young gentleman who, when entertaining in his bachelor flat, offers asparagus. This might at first seem an admirable choice; not only is it fool-proof to cook, but it is expensive— (even when it comes from the deep freeze)—and may therefore be regarded as a flattering compliment. A moment's reflection should convince him of the folly of such reasoning. Asparagus must be served with hot melted butter, and though many lip-sticks are 'kiss-proof' they are not butter-proof. Apart from this elemental disadvantage it is impossible for a young lady, while absorbing asparagus, to retain any suggestion of feminine allure. She has to hold back her head and stick out her elbow and open wide her mouth, and these three actions, when performed simultaneously, are the reverse of romantic.

Young ladies are not often so misguided, though I do know of one case where a very promising affair was killed stone dead because the girl began dinner by serving corn-on-the-cob. No choice could have been more disastrous. The young man, who was an amateur boxer, had an entire set of false teeth, and declined the dish without explaining why he was obliged to do so. This greatly offended her; the dinner was a flop from the word one, and they did not even reach the coffee stage. All of which was much to be regretted for the young man, in all but dental respects, was extremely well-equipped, and anyway she would have found out sooner or later.

Here is an ideal menu for the modern Romeo and Juliet, with Juliet playing the part of hostess. Juliet, by the way, lives in a small Chelsea flat with a tiny kitchen. She has a reasonably well-paid job which enables her to be home at 6 if she catches the right bus. Romeo is coming to dinner at 7, so everything will have to be prepared in advance.

Incidentally, we will assume that Juliet is a sensible girl who has no illusions about Romeo's intentions. In these days the definition of a 'sensible girl' differs somewhat from the image of my youth. In those distant days, a sensible girl was one who, having entered a taxi on the way home from the theatre, froze like a jelly, slid over to the other side, and stifled further conversation by observing that Ivor Novello was quite marvellous, wasn't he.

Times have changed. Juliet will be prepared for some form of dalliance and presumably will welcome it. This does not mean that she must put on black silk slacks and be discovered upside down on the divan. But it does mean that dalliance will be in the air. I should begin with . . .

Hot consommé. Romeo will not be fooled by the idea that she has made it herself, but he will be impressed by the fact that Juliet can make even tinned consommé exciting, which she can, by spicing it with a liqueur glass of sherry, adding a liberal dash of Worcester sauce, and serving it in an earthenware bowl with a handful of devilled almonds in the saucer, dusted with cayenne.

After this fiery opening we come to the main dish, and here I have very definite opinions. I think that it should be cold, waiting on the sideboard, for nothing so quickly destroys a romantic atmosphere as constantly popping in and out of the kitchen, putting on aprons and taking them off again, etc., etc. I also think that it should be home-made. No plates of tongue, even if they are tarted up with parsley, no slabs of veal-and-ham pie. Romeo can get that sort of thing at the snack bar of his local pub, every day of his life, and probably does.

There are, of course, a thousand cold dishes which Juliet could prepare for such an occasion, but since we are limited to one, I shall settle for . . .

Mousse of Crab

My main reason for choosing this dish is that it will give Romeo ideas. Not in the aphrodisiac sense; it does not dilate the nostrils nor quicken the pulse nor cause the breath to come in quick short pants. The ideas it evokes are subtler, but likely to be more enduring. For as it glides gently down his gullet Romeo—temporarily averting his eyes from the divan . . . may well say to himself . . . 'If she can do this sort of thing on twenty-five pounds a week what could she do on sixty-five, which is what we should have if we joined up?' And as he takes another gulp he may well begin to see visions of the future, particularly if Juliet has proffered him a glass of white wine. (Spanish, from the off-licence, properly chilled at 75p a bottle.) Visions of a rise in salary, a little house, a dinner for the boss, at which she will look enchanting. Those visions which, though sentimental and old-hat, are still, happily, inclined to flit through the imaginations of the young.

Here is the recipe for this delicious thing, which, though it is inexpensive and simple to make, would not be out of place on a cold buffet at the Ritz.

Mousse of Crab

1 tin Cornish crab (or lobster) soup
$\frac{1}{4}$ pint cream
$\frac{1}{4}$ lb peeled prawns
1 white of egg, beaten stiff
1 tablespoonful mayonnaise*
1 envelope gelatine
Seasoning. Salt, pepper, mace, garlic.

Mix soup, prawns, cream and mayonnaise in blender.
Fold in white of egg.
Dissolve gelatine in cup of hot water, and mix in, after
seasoning to taste.
Allow to set. Decorate to taste, e.g., with a little circle
of prawns in the centre, and a sprinkling of finely
chopped chives.

This is a rather rich dish so I usually give it a tang of
sharpness by serving it with a salad of iced cucumber.
Well salted, of course, and drained, so that it is pleasantly
limp. Raw unsalted cucumber is one of those dishes that
should be seen and not heard. Unfortunately it usually *is*
heard, shortly after dinner, in a series of discreetly muffled
bleeps from those guests who have partaken too freely
of it.

And the finale? (Always assuming that this blend of
sensuous charm has not yet propelled them both to the
divan.) For the last course, I think, Juliet should play safe,
and curb her girlish inclination to offer a sweet.

The reason for this is entirely psychological. One of
the most firmly held convictions of the masculine animal
is that men—real men—do not hanker after sweets. In
fact they hanker after them like mad. If you wander past

* I will not insult Juliet by reminding her that this must be home-
made. If she is the sort of girl who uses bottled mayonnaise she
should give up cooking altogether, and take Romeo out to dinner
for a cold sausage at the King's Head. For a note on mayonnaise
see page 196 ff.

a building site at lunch-time—(and it is always lunch-time on building sites, which is the main reason for the housing shortage)—you will see hairy giants creeping away into corners and devouring chocolate biscuits in a positive frenzy. Men love sweets—but, for some strange reason, they seem to have decided that sweets are not to be associated with masculine virility, which is what they all aspire to. In the same context a great many quite normal men love small Siamese kittens, Chopin nocturnes played with the soft pedal on, and the sound of the wind in the willows. But not in public.

Should it be a cheese board? No. Unless the board has a selection of at least six cheeses it looks rather dreary, and even six cheeses, at present prices, 'mount up'. A cream cheese sprinkled with sugar might do, but because of the aforesaid image of masculine virility it is best avoided. So I recommend . . .

Devilled Eggs

Hard boil 4 eggs, leave them to cool, remove from shell and cut them in halves. Take out the yolks, very carefully, so that you do not damage the whites. Mix two tablespoons of double cream with a teaspoon of English mustard and a very generous dash of Worcester sauce. Mash the yolks into this incendiary concoction, and when it is smooth, arrange it in the whites and take it to the larder. Do *not* put it into the refrigerator.

Postscript

Sometimes, when one has published a book of a controversial nature, it is a good idea to go to a public library and borrow it oneself, in order to see if readers have been scribbling comments in the margins. I have done this on several occasions, with somewhat deflating results. 'Rubbish!' 'Tripe!' 'Doesn't know what he is talking about!' Those are the pencilled accusations which one must be prepared for, together with a great many marks of exclamation . . . !!!! . . . and of interrogation . . . ????

When this book is published it is a fairly safe bet that similar comments will be scribbled against the present chapter, which is nothing if not controversial. Indeed, the few women to whom I have shown it have disagreed with it quite vehemently. Never mind. Women, like children, seldom know what is best for themselves.

However, some of these critics did come up with interesting ideas. Several of them, for instance, suggested that I had omitted to mention the most obvious sexual culinary device of all . . . the chafing-dish. Chafing-dishes, they suggested, are ideally contrived for two people. The dish sits in the middle of the table, and the little violet flame casts pretty shadows on a girl's face. It provides something to talk about when conversation flags, and if Romeo shows an absolutely uncontrollable urge towards the divan, the flame can be puffed out, and relit when the calls of romance have been satisfied.

Yes, there is a great deal to be said for chafing-dishes, and we should rid ourselves of the idea that their uses are confined to such unenterprising projects as hotting up cocktail sausages or making mushroom omelettes. You can cook almost anything in a chafing-dish—except, of course, those dishes that need to be put in the oven. You can grill, you can stew, you can fry, you can even boil. And while you are cooking you can still look reasonably alluring.

Perhaps the only way in which we shall ever arrive at a satisfactory answer to the problem of Cookery and Sex is through a National Opinion Poll. If the women were honest, the results might be fascinating. I can visualize the winning titles. 'I Won His Heart with a Haddock.' That might arouse a faint interest. 'Meat and Man Appeal.' Getting warmer. 'The Curry that Changed my Life.' Warmer still.

With a consolation prize for 'We just sat and talked'.

CHAPTER 12

The Ice Age

Pterodactyl Soup
Casserole of Mammoth
Dodos' Eggs on Toast

THIS menu, under various disguises, is frequently served in the restaurant cars of British Rail, but its neolithic quality is due, not to the ingredients, but to the chef. Railway chefs have a genius for 'antiquing' their food, and can be guaranteed to transform a quite ordinary lamb chop into something that tastes as though it had been carved, in distant ages, from the hindquarters of a sabre-toothed tiger.

As it happens, the menu—in theory at any rate—would be quite practical, provided that a sufficient number of intrepid explorers, armed with the necessary equipment, could delve deep enough into the frozen secrets of the past. There is no limit—so science-fiction magazines inform us—to the span of time over which food can be preserved in a state fit for human consumption. In theory, there is nothing to prevent a suburban housewife from concocting a salad from the fronds of ferns that have long vanished from the pages of botanical history, flaked with the fins of sharks that were swimming in perilous seas long before Man was thought of. Admittedly, she would need a deep-freeze the size of the Albert Hall, and after preparing her collation she would almost certainly expire, partly from frost-bite and partly from indigestion. But it could be done.

The advent of the Ice Age, which in Britain is still comparatively in its infancy, has for me a special fascination because I am old enough to remember the days when home-made ice-cream was still a startling novelty. I was eight years old when I first tasted it, and it was served to me in bed as a special treat, when I was recovering from an attack of measles. The whole household was involved in its manufacture, which was centred in a large wooden bucket containing a cylinder of tin. The mixture, prepared by my mother, was poured into the tin, which was then surrounded by chunks of ice purchased from the fishmonger's and delivered by an errand boy on his bicycle. The ice-blocks were sprinkled with rock-salt to prevent them from freezing too rapidly, and as soon as everything was in readiness, my brothers took it in turns to crank a handle attached to a device which agitated the slowly thickening mixture in the tin. The whole thing took nearly an hour, but it was worth it. When the first spoonful was scooped out and handed to me on a plate, all eyes were fixed upon me and there was silence in the bedroom while I tasted it. A taste, or rather a sensation, that I shall never forget, the sharp tang of the cream as it touched my tongue and the delicious sensation as it slid down my throat. Even to this day, I still feel there is something exotic and slightly avant-garde about ice-cream, especially when it is served in a private house—a feeling that could never be shared by modern infants.

Back to the dinner table. There is no easier, prettier, nicer or more generally satisfactory sweet than the fruit ice-creams which you can nowadays buy, packed in their original skins, from the deep-freeze people. When you put them on the table they look like a set of delicate Chelsea china. However, if you buy new ones every time they are expensive, so it is better to buy fresh oranges, lemons, or what-have-you, scoop out the fruit, and put the skins into the deep-freeze where they will last for weeks. As for the ice itself, there is a wide range of sorbets, packed in large containers, from which you scoop out the required amount as the occasion requires.

A word of warning for those who have not yet been initiated into the marvels of the Ice Age. These ice-creams melt very rapidly and should not be removed from the freezer until ten minutes before they are eaten.

I bought my freezer on the spur of the moment, which is the best—indeed, the only way—to buy anything which costs rather a lot of money. It is only when you are trying to do something economical, like buying cheap ties at a sale, that you should pause and give the matter thought. If you pause long enough, and think hard enough, the ties—hopefully—will all have been snatched up by somebody else before you have made up your mind, whereupon you can walk out of the shop and return to Bond Street.

My freezer, which cost £98, is called a Bosch; and when it arrived there were the usual alarms as to whether it would explode. These alarms are a purely personal trait, inherited from a stormy childhood in which even inanimate objects were invested with an aura of fear. As it happens, even to comparatively normal people, the occasional sounds emitted by the Bosch, though muffled and discreet, have an eerie quality, particularly when one is not prepared for them. One is standing in the kitchen, with an onion in one hand and a cookery book in the other, when suddenly from the larder there comes a low purring vibration, as though an immense cat had prowled through the door and were sniffing round the shelves. Needless to say, this only means that the machine has decided that it is not cold enough, and is switching back the freezing mechanisms. But it does suggest that the machine has a mind of its own, and in this there is an element of the uncanny. After a time, one gets used to it.

The only thing that exploded, as far as the Bosch was concerned, was the first thing that I ever put into it. This was a bottle of champagne, which was intended to be drunk in celebration of the occasion. I had forgotten the expansive propensities of frozen liquids, and when I went to take out the bottle I discovered that it had burst, and that the tray was covered with a curious ectoplasmic heap of frozen wine. This, when placed between the teeth and crunched, was quite delicious.

My other alarm concerned the electricity account. All this purring and growling, although it was almost inaudible, would it not mean that my next electricity bill would reach astronomical proportions? The answer, fortunately, was in the negative. Indeed, thanks to various other economies for which the freezer has been responsible, the electricity bills have actually gone down.

Although Bejam, the largest frozen food business in Britain, was founded only five years ago, it already has stores all over the South of England, catering for a quarter of a million customers, which suggests that the Ice Age is here to stay. Let us pay a visit to our local branch.

In doing so, we have a feeling that we are stepping into a new world—a feeling which, in my case, is enhanced by the fact that I am stepping out of a very old one. I leave my cottage (circa 1790) and head for Richmond Park, which was laid out in the eighteenth century by the first of the great English landscape gardeners, 'Capability' Brown. I drive through groves of ancient oaks, with the deer dancing through the bracken, and then, as I pass through the gates, the suburbs begin, and in a few minutes I am parking the car in the shadow of a skyscraper.

As I push through the swing-doors, and begin to wend my way through the long lines of white metal freezers, something rather strange happens. My eyes are drawn, not to the titles of the contents—Fish, Poultry, Vegetables, etc.—but to the customers, mostly women. It would be perhaps too fanciful to suggest that there is such a thing as a 'Bejam Woman'. Such a creature would evoke disturbing visions of pre-history, like the Pitcairn man. But I do maintain that there is a type who may, without exaggeration, be described as a 'Deep-Freeze Woman', not because she appears to be emotionally frigid, or in any way inhuman, but because her desires are pre-set, her needs are catalogued, and she cannot be swayed or softened from her resolutions. She knows what she wants—(note the list of food-items which she clutches in her hand)—she knows that she can get it, and she gets it.

Admittedly, there are a few exceptions to this rule—I suspect that they are newcomers—who drift about in the same haphazard way as Supermarket Women. These women greatly annoy me because they have a habit of opening the lids of the freezers and peering at the contents in a sort of daze, as though they were watching a peep-show. I feel like going up to them and saying, 'Darlings, do make up your minds; one piece of frozen cod is exactly the same as another piece of frozen cod; and if you keep the lid open much longer everything will begin to melt.' This, as it happens, would not be strictly true; if you buy frozen food and take it home in the specially insulated bags provided for this purpose, it will come to no harm for a couple of hours.

Here is a story about cod which, until I got a deep-freeze, was a fish I was apt to despise. During the war a friend of mine was serving in a mine-sweeper and one day a mine went off and the whole sea erupted with cod, which were splattered all over the decks. (Not a technical description but you know what I mean.) The cod were immediately cooked for the crew and were quite delicious. This, mutatis mutandis, is what happens in the case of deep-freeze cod. As soon as the wretched creatures are caught, they are frozen stiff. No time lag, no train-journeys, no sad interludes on a marble slab. This is why deep-freeze cod, in my opinion, are far superior to the things you buy in the fish shop.

Here is a recipe for Cod au Gratin, for the exclusive use of deep-freeze addicts.

Thaw 1½ lbs of fish, cut into slices, and place in a fireproof dish that has been generously buttered.

Grate 3 ounces of cheese. It need not be Parmesan, which is expensive. Any old rat-trap variety will do.

Melt 1 ounce of butter and 1 ounce of flour; add 1 level teaspoon of dry mustard and crush a garlic clove over the mixture which, as you go on stirring it, will gradually form itself into a sort of ball.

Still stirring, slowly pour in ½ pint of milk, and bring to a gentle boil.

Finally, add 2 ounces of the cheese, salt and pepper to taste, and pour the whole thing over the fish.

When it has settled down, sprinkle with the last ounce of the cheese and dust with breadcrumbs.

It is now ready for the oven, where it should bake at a medium heat for not less than 20 minutes and not more than half an hour.

The Ice Age has brought about such a revolution, not only in the art of cookery but in the over-all nourishment of mankind's millions, that in order to envisage its potentialities one would need a brain combining the most salient qualities of Jules Verne, H. G. Wells, Henry Ford and Fanny Cradock. I do not share their talents—though it would be nice to think that one had something in common with Fanny. I can only sit, and wait, and wonder what will come next.

There will be disappointments, of course. One must not succumb to the delusion that the deep-freeze contains the answer to all the complex problems of domestic economy. Anybody who has ever been rash enough to try to deep-freeze a tomato or a lettuce will agree that the results are uneatable. As a general rule one should assume that the higher the water content of the object to be frozen the less satisfactory will be results. Cucumbers, which are 97 per cent water, emerge from the freezer like rocks and rapidly degenerate into a mass of exceptionally repulsive slime.

One has to learn these things by experiment. However, a great deal of trouble and money can be saved by consulting the experts, and studying some of the new cookery books which have emerged in the wake of this scientific revolution. Some of those that I have read have left me feeling more than faintly refrigerated myself, because their writers seem to be more interested in temperature than in taste, but if you persevere you will eventually find what you want.*

Meanwhile here are some autobiographical jottings which may illustrate how the freezer has widened my own horizons. And though it may seem odd to begin with potted shrimps—which are not usually associated with horizon-widening—I make no apologies for doing so, because it was through the medium of this excellent and essentially English delicacy that I first came to realize that the Ice Age had come to stay.

* The best book of deep-freeze cookery that I have yet encountered is *Deep Freeze Cookery* by Marika Hanbury Tenison (MacGibbon and Kee, 1971, £3.20). It is so simple, so comprehensive, and so intelligently written that it is worthy of study even by those who have not yet invested in deep-freezers.

I had owned the freezer for over a year before it was necessary to defrost it. The manufacturers suggest that this should be done every six months, but in mechanical matters I have always gone on the principle that if a thing is working it is wise to leave it alone till it falls to pieces. However, the day came when everything in the freezer was beginning to stick together in a gelid mass, so I turned off the switch and awaited the thaw. Meanwhile I telephoned to various friends who were pleased, though puzzled, to learn that they were about to receive presents of chickens and legs of lamb.

When the thaw was complete the last thing to be removed was an object wrapped in foil that I had entirely forgotten about. On removing the foil it was revealed as a dish of potted shrimps which had been lurking there for over a year. The immediate reaction was to take it out and put it on the compost heap. Then I remembered that we were living in the Ice Age, so I kept it, and served it for dinner two days later, when it was greeted with loud applause. It was delicious, and the shrimps tasted as fresh as if one had just fished them out of the sea at Morecambe Bay.

Here is the recipe, for four persons. (This method of preparing them differs in several important respects from most standard recipes, including Constance Spry's.)

Buy 1 lb of packet shrimps, peeled and cooked. (The shrimp people have a habit of calling them 'prawns', but I have never been able to discover the difference.)

Have ready, on the draining board . . .

Two saucepans
$\frac{1}{2}$ lb of butter
1 heaped teaspoon ground mace
1 heaped teaspoon freshly ground pepper
1 heaped tablespoonful squashed garlic
1 coffeespoon cayenne pepper
1 wooden spoon

1 'receptacle', preferably a shallow dish of earthenware. This is a pleasantly plebeian delicacy, which would look ill-at-ease if associated with your best Meissen.

Pause.

Close all doors and windows to ensure that there are no feline intrusions. Cats can scent shrimps from far afield, and have even been known to descend chimneys when they suspect that anything concerning shrimps is in the air.

Resumption. (Here the tempo accelerates.)

Drain shrimps, which have a tiresome habit of weeping.

Cut butter in half, putting $\frac{1}{4}$ lb into saucepan A and $\frac{1}{4}$ lb into saucepan B.

Turn on gas, melt butter gently in saucepan A, add seasoning, put in shrimps, stirring with the wooden spoon, heat through, but do not let them sauter.

Melt other butter in saucepan B, rather more quickly, and when it stops foaming, 'clarify' it, which is simply a snooty way of saying skim off the top.

Give shrimps a final stir, pour on clarified butter from saucepan B, press the surface flat. And that is the end of the operation, except to wait for them to cool, to carry them to the deep-freeze, and to open the doors and the windows in order to readmit the cats who will almost certainly have been waiting outside in a state of understandable frustration.

Chocolates

Deep-frozen chocolates are delicious, particularly those flat pepperminty chocolates which one sometimes serves with the coffee. Needless to say, one does not keep them in too long, or they will be hurtful to those whose dental equipment is showing signs of wear. Fifteen minutes is enough. But those fifteen minutes make all the difference. The chocolate acquires a faintly crunchy quality and the peppermints taste pleasantly sharp.

Baked Potatoes with Savoury Fillings

The trouble about baked potatoes, particularly if you live alone, and only want one potato at a time, is the gas bill. Perhaps my oven is temperamental but I find that a good-sized potato needs at least two hours, which uses a great deal of gas. With a freezer you can cook a dozen together, or a hundred, if you feel so inclined.

Assuming that you have cooked the potatoes, sliced off the tops, scooped out the centres, and mashed them in a bowl with a *minimum* of butter, the savoury filling is a matter of taste. My own preference is very simple—a lacing of grated Parmesan cheese and a single pungent herb, such as sage. If you are more ambitious you can add sour cream and chips of crisp bacon and chives, but if you go on adding things you will end up by feeling like Fanny Cradock doing a star turn at the Albert Hall.

The real object of the exercise is to have a constant supply of baked potatoes, pre-cooked and ready to serve in an emergency.

To freeze, you merely wrap them in foil and forget about them.

To thaw, you put them in a hot oven for 20 minutes. And that is that.

Footnote for Funerals

The whole conception of deep-freeze cookery is so rich in possibilities that I cannot help feeling that the day will come when it will be employed for purposes and occasions which have not yet been envisaged. One of these occasions, surely, would be a funeral, where the guests partook of a meal that had actually been cooked and frozen by the dear departed. There would be no cause for tears, indeed, it might be quite a festive event, particularly if the deceased had been a good cook. Nor would there be any need for melancholy in the choice of the menu, which might well begin with some form of vol-au-vent (we are assuming that the dear departed prided herself on her pastry). Yes—a vol-au-vent would be eminently suitable. And should any literary persons be present, as they might well be at my own demise, it would give them a happy chance of displaying their erudition. As soon as the delicacy touched their lips they could pause, and sigh, and murmur 'Oh, for the touch of a vanished hand!'

My Cup of Tea

ONE of the most vivid memories of my child-hood was the look of horror which froze my mother's face when—on one of her at-home days —the house-parlourmaid, staggering under the weight of a heavily loaded silver tea-tray, appeared at the door of the drawing-room wearing elbow-sleeves.

This sentence is so rich in Edwardian nostalgia that it may be incomprehensible to some modern readers. We will elucidate.

'At-home days.' These were convenient social conventions for the impoverished Edwardian gentlewoman. They implied that on certain definite afternoons of the month she would be pleased to receive her friends and neighbours, between certain hours, and that on all the other afternoons of the month, she would be 'out' . . . (which meant lurking in the shrubbery or peering through the bedroom window, to see who was ringing the front-door bell). If you were well-off you were 'at home' once a week; if you were very poor, once a month; if you were betwixt and between, once a fortnight. Hence the legend on my mother's visiting cards . . .

Mrs John Nichols

First and Third Tuesdays   *Cleave Court*

Torquay

If such a piece of pasteboard were included in one of those capsules which are occasionally buried in remote places by historians, with the object of informing future generations about the customs of the twentieth century, I wonder what they would make of it? They might possibly decide that they had stumbled upon the evidence of some obscure religious rite. In this conclusion they would have been correct. The 'at-home' days *were* religious rites, strictly ruled and regulated, with the silver tea-pot as an object of worship in the centre of the ceremonies.

'House-Parlourmaid.' This is another phrase which the modern reader may find mysterious; it is typical of the sort of Edwardian middle-class snobbery which has mercifully vanished from the world.

A 'house-parlourmaid' was a reliable indication of her employer's income bracket—between £1,000 and £1,500 a year. If you were rich, which in those days meant anything from £4,000 a year upwards, you had a butler, a parlourmaid, a house-maid, a cook, and a 'tweeny'. ('Tweenies' were pathetic and rather squashed-looking girls who hovered about in the kitchens getting in everybody's way.) If you were 'comfortable' on, say, £2,500 a year, you had a house-maid, a parlourmaid and a cook. But when you sank below these levels, and when two maids were beyond your capacity, you had to be content with a 'house-parlourmaid'. Even as a boy, I found the phrase depressing, for it seemed to suggest a social status to which we had no entitlement. However, to my mother, and indeed to all impoverished Edwardian

158

gentlewomen, it was a phrase that helped to reinforce the numerous fictions that enabled us to 'keep up appearances'. It was a proof that we had not yet sunk to the lowest depths, where you could only afford a 'general'. We did, indeed, sink to these depths at one time, but our 'general' was so efficient, and my mother took such pains to see that she was smartly dressed, with her aprons and caps meticulously ironed, that the visitors to our at-home days may have thought that she was actually a real whole-time parlour-maid.

Elbow-sleeves. What about them? Were they the symbol of some strange revolutionary movement, in which the acolytes rose against the aristocrats, and the foundations of the establishment were undermined?

Yes, they were, but it would take too long to explain why. It is enough to say that our house-parlourmaid, whom we spot-lit in the drawing-room door, was an Edwardian sex-symbol, even though she was staggering under the weight of the tea-tray. In her tiny bedroom, on her £30 a year, she had suddenly decided to revolt. If 'ladies' could wear elbow-sleeves—(which simply meant sleeves cut short at the elbow)—if 'ladies' could so shamelessly expose themselves in the day-time, with inflammatory effects upon the emotions of the opposite sex, so could she. And she did, but not for long. My mother, needless to say, was obliged to give her a week's notice.

This picture of an Edwardian tea-table might seem to have no place in a volume such as this, but I insert it because, through the symbol of tea, it offers us a unique reminder of the immense social changes of the last fifty years. Indeed, we need not go back as far as that, for the rituals of the tea-table were still widely observed throughout our country until the outbreak of the Second World War, not only by the middle classes, but also, and perhaps especially, by the aristocracy.

The grandest, most formidable, most glittering, and

altogether most impressive tea-table at which I occasionally seated myself was at Polesden-Lacey, the home of Mrs Ronnie Greville—whom we have met before. Gossip writers often described her, somewhat maliciously, as 'the power behind a throne'—a title that was not without some justification, for she was affectionately regarded by many members of the Royal Family. But it was not only in the royal connotation that Maggie exercised her influence. She was an ardent patriot—as she interpreted patriotism—which really meant that she rejoiced in the amount of red blotches with which our early Empire builders had spattered the maps of the world. And though it was not within her power to appoint ministers or bestow offices, her capacity for intrigue was limitless and she used her substantial riches with startling effect. At about the time I met her there was much speculation as to who would be the next Viceroy of India and it was generally considered that Lord Lloyd, who had greatly distinguished himself in Egypt, was the most likely candidate. Maggie thought otherwise. Although he might have shone in Egypt he had certainly failed to shine at Polesden, on his first and only visit there. She had set him at the bridge-table in a foursome which included the Queen of Spain, who had rashly gone a grand slam in spades. Lord Lloyd had promptly doubled her; she had redoubled; and the result, for Spain, was disastrous. All very tiresome, and the man, obviously, was not quite a gentleman. I can still hear her voice as she later described to me the outcome of this unfortunate incident. 'There was a time,' she purred, 'when George Lloyd thought he might get India. But I soon put a stop to *that*.'

Back to the tea-table. Tea is at 5 o'clock, and at Polesden 5 o'clock means 5 o'clock and not 5 minutes past. Which in its turn means that the Spanish ambassador, who has gone for a walk down the yew avenue, hastily retraces his steps, and that the Chancellor of the Exchequer, whoever he may be, hurries down the great staircase, followed by several members of the House of Lords, and that the various ladies belonging to these gentlemen rise from the chaises-longues on which they have been resting in their bedrooms, removing the perfumed anti-wrinkle pads which they have been balancing on their foreheads, and join the procession to the tea-table which is set out in one of the smaller drawing-rooms.

It is a pity that no artist, as far as I am aware, ever painted a picture of that tea-table, for it is rich in charming detail. The tea-pots, the cream-jugs, the milk-pots, and the sugar-basins are of Queen Anne silver; the tea-service is Meissen; and the doyleys, heavily mono-grammed, are of Chantilly lace. The tea is Indian, China, and a special brew which Maggie described as 'Lord Reading's special'. (He once proposed to her.) The cream has been extracted from some very expensive breed of cow on the home-farm. It is so thick that Americans have been known to mistake it for custard. The scones are piping hot, some of them flavoured with cinnamon; the bread-and-butter is paper thin, and the buttered toast so lavishly buttered that you have to be careful that it does not spill onto your trousers. As for the cakes . . . These have been created, the day before, by Maggie's chef in her immense kitchens, and they are really quite something. Towers of coffee cream, meringues, petits fours, etc., etc. Since we have already eaten a very large lunch and will shortly be eating an even larger dinner—(prefaced by sherry and croutons of caviar at eight o'clock) —it might be supposed that few of the guests would have much appetite for these delicacies, but they present so alluring an appearance that they are eagerly devoured, particularly if Royalty are present, because—as Maggie learned in the days of dear King Edward—Royalty is apt to have a sweet tooth. And it would be terrible if Queen Mary, having graciously accepted one of the meringues, were to find that she was the only person eating them. A a sort of lèse majesté.

All this is a very long way from the age of the tea-bag, popped into the pot by 'mum' in the Council house when the 'kiddies' come home—a very long way from tea in the factory, gushing out of an urn, or even from tea on the telly, where it is presented against glamorous backgrounds, being sipped by exquisitely moulded young goddesses, as though there were some mystique about it. Well, perhaps there *is* a mystique about it. For in spite of the social and historical gap between tea at Polesden and tea in the Council house, there is a common denominator linking these two ceremonies—and that is the tea itself. The warmth of it, the scent of it, the tang of it, the curious, subtle, insinuating comfort of it. The rites at Polesden, the customs of the Council house, could not have been celebrated in any language but the language of tea.

What were the secrets of this language?

To answer this question, we must change the scene.

Some five thousand years ago—so legend has it—a few leaves from a wild bush fell accidentally into a pot of water that was being boiled for the Chinese Emperor Shen Nung. If this were a film script we should see a panorama of surprising pictures in the fragrant steam that drifted from his cup. We should see fleets of ships sailing the seven seas, see great buildings rising to the skies, the rise and fall of economic empires, see the smoke of war. All because a vagrant wind tossed a few leaves into an Emperor's tea cup. This, at least, is the legend, and since legends are often nearer to the truth than the most meticulously documented history, we may care to believe it.

Among the visions that we should see is the vast layout of buildings that make up the headquarters of J. Lyons and Company to which we will now resort. I have visited many industrial complexes in a journalistic capacity, and my main feeling at the end of the tour has been one of sympathy for those royal persons who have to spend so large a part of their lives factory-visiting. Nothing is more fatiguing than being obliged to assume an intelligent interest in masses of noisy equipment about which one knows nothing and cares less, and it must be exceptionally agonizing to be obliged to do this while one is clutching clumps of wilting carnations and blinking against the flash-lights.

But a tea-factory bears little resemblance to these infernos, and even when there is noise, the senses are soothed by the all-pervading scent of tea, which seems to drift into every corner. The fragrance is most potent in the Tasting Room, which might be compared to a sort of laboratory of the senses, though when one first enters it, and is confronted by the long vistas of gleaming white tables, on which are displayed hundreds of cups of mysterious sepia fluids, one might be excused for thinking that one had strayed into a chapel of the space age, and interrupted some weird religious ceremony.

This impression of an exotic ritual is heightened by a curious and rather intimidating sound echoing constantly through the chamber, which is otherwise hushed. It is the sound which comes from the back of the throats of the high priests of the ceremonial—the tea-tasters— as they suck in spoonfuls of the blend they are sampling, and then, with a mixture of a gargle and an expectoration, eject it into metal spittoons.

This, one must admit, is a remarkable way of earning a living, but a very profitable one. Really expert tea-tasters would turn up their noses at the salaries of really expert cabinet ministers—(if such persons exist, which is open to question).

Judging from those whom I have had the pleasure of meeting, they earn their money. Their sense of taste is so delicate that it acquires an almost psychic quality, and this quality has developed, over the years, its own vocabulary, which would be incomprehensible to the uninitiated. In assessing their teas they use such words as 'thickness' and 'nerve' and even 'bone'. (That is a startling expression. Who would have suspected that tea might have a 'bone' in it?) Some of the tea-tasters, when you get to know them, lapse into the language of the wine-tasters, and wax eloquent over tea that is 'dry' or 'mellow' or 'pungent' or 'sharp' or 'full-bodied'.

Yes—they earn their money. Some of them have to do this gargle-expectoration act a thousand times a day. And while they are doing it they have to keep their senses alert, balancing the flower-taste of Ceylon against the malt-and-honey taste of Assam, studying charts of statistics from a multitude of Eastern estates and—as if that were not enough—keeping their eye on the world markets, which are in a perpetual state of flux.

Tea-tasters, I fancy, must make good husbands. They must be sensitive to mood, to flavour, and to fragrance; and most wives, surely, must wish these qualities to be appreciated. Apart from all that, they bring home the money.

Tea plays a very large part in the lives of the British people, who consume twenty-five per cent of the entire world output. Sometimes one might feel that it plays almost too large a part, particularly when it infuses itself into the scripts of the television dramatists. Tea, in television drama, has become a sort of nervous twitch. When the door flings open, to reveal a blood-spattered juvenile delinquent or a pregnant daughter, the action is invariably held up until somebody—usually 'Mum' or 'Dad'—has put the kettle on.

For this reason it seems strange that so few women know how to make it. We will now inform them.

Here is the recipe for the perfect cup. The basic

rules are childishly simple, but they are not always observed.

Some women do not even bother to warm the pot. We will avert our eyes from such creatures, and stick to the rules.

1. A few seconds before the kettle comes to the boil, empty the hot water from the pot, put in one teaspoon per person—(no nonsense about 'one extra for the pot')—lift the pot to the kettle—(in that order, *not* the kettle to the pot)—and then, the instant the water boils, pour it onto the tea.
2. Leave it to stand for 2 minutes, and then stir—preferably with a wooden spoon. Leave for one more minute. It is then ready to serve. Whereupon . . .
3. Pour in the milk. Pour it in *before* the tea.

Here we enter the realm of etiquette, with nostalgic memories of Nancy Mitford who—though she was otherwise a sensible woman, and though she was born into very respectable circles, spread the strangest ideas about what was done, and what was not done, by the upper classes. One did not use the word 'mirror' said Nancy. It must be 'looking-glass'. But one did use the word 'mirror', and one still does, and one always should, as Shakespeare would be the first to agree. Nor, said Nancy, should one speak of a mantelpiece. It must be 'chimney-piece'. The odd thing about her was that she really felt that these things were important, and, as a result of her crusading zeal, she also persuaded a lot of silly people to follow her example.

The reason for putting in the milk first—according to our friends the tea-tasters—is that if cold milk is poured onto hot tea the milk is scalded. It is a very sensitive fluid, and it just does not care for that sort of shock.

Another Nancy Mitford aversion was the tea-bag. I was once sitting with her in the shade of a cabano on the Venetian Lido next to a bogus Italian princess who was giving a tea-party of great distinction, with a footman in attendance. As soon as the footman had poured the hot water into the cups the princess thrust out a scarlet-clawed hand and plopped in a tea-bag. Nancy found this very distressing. Tea-bags, she observed, in her exceptionally upper-class voice, reminded her of contraceptives. (Which she called contraceptivos.) I remember agreeing with her, adding that a tea-bag contraceptivo in these circumstances would be not only inelegant but dangerous, as it would almost certainly be covered with sand.

However, the Mitford tea-bag aversion has no scientific backing, which is fortunate for the shareholders of Lyons and Co., who produce no less than 5,600 tea-bags every minute (*sic*). Tea from tea-bags is just as good as tea from silver spoons. And should you happen to be repelled by them when they have fulfilled their functions and when you drop the soggy things into the sink . . . and should you feel as though you were dealing with a collection of wet bathing-pants recently discarded by a team of negro midgets . . . that is your own affair. It is the way you were brought up.

I was not brought up on tea-bags, but I was certainly brought up—socially—round the tea-table, because in our family there was seldom enough money to justify the expense of giving a luncheon party. As for dinners, they were quite out of the question. Tea it was, and tea it had to be. And although we have already caught a glimpse of our little provincial Edwardian tea-table I should like to pay it a brief return visit, if only to capture a few thistledown memories of a vanished age, before they fly 'over the hills and far away'.

There was always mulberry jam. This, in my opinion, is the most delicious jam ever invented, particularly if it is served with thick dollops of Devonshire cream. The mulberries came from an ancient tree that cast long shadows over the tennis lawn, and during the holidays I used to be sent out to pick them after they had fallen onto the grass. When I came back with a basketful I usually had a very fair imitation of Keats' purple-stained mouth, and in all probability might have been heard whispering snatches of the ode to a nightingale as I went into the kitchen. Very early in life, as an exceptionally frightened little boy—and with good reason—I discovered that a little Keats, learned by heart, was an excellent sedative when the devil was around, as, in our home, he usually was.

You make mulberry jam in the same way as raspberry or strawberry jam, though I think that it is given an extra tang by the addition of lemon rind. The only problem about it is where to find the mulberries. Although they are among the longest lived trees in nature—(there is one at Christ's College, Cambridge, under which Milton is supposed to have sat)—they are hard to come by. The late twentieth century, alas, is not the age of the mulberry tree; they need space to stretch their finely muscled arms; they also need slaves to tend them, to guard them against the assaults of the hosts of insects for whom they have a special attraction. (They are always, of course, the first choice of silkworms when they are studying the menu.) And though the late twentieth century is certainly an age of slaves, the slaves are all doing the wrong things. Instead of tending lawns, and bathing ducal babies, and curtseying to ladies of the manor as they sweep through the porches of country churches—all of which is very good for the complexion—they have chosen to rivet themselves to factory benches, deafened by the noise of infernal machines, at enormous expense not only to the community but to their deluded selves. None of which is in any way beneficial to the complexion.

End of recipe for mulberry jam.

And the other essentials? Well, in summer there were

always cucumber sandwiches, and sometimes I think that a cucumber sandwich, rampant, would be a pleasing and decorative addition to the heraldic symbols of our sceptred isle. The cucumbers came from the only one of our greenhouses that had not fallen into total disrepair. Another sandwich was made from a delicious paste called Patum Peperium, which was only bought for special occasions. It came in an elegant white jar, with the sub-title 'Gentleman's Relish'. There were always several cakes, and the condition of the family fortunes could be judged by their quality. When things were not too bad I would be sent into Torquay on my bicycle to buy a Fuller's walnut layer cake which, miraculously, has sur-vived over the years, and can still be bought from the same firm, though at a somewhat different price. When things were not too good, I would be told to buy a nine-penny 'household' cake, which was a sort of inferior plum, and a 'German' cake, which was a sponge with a filling of lemon cream. On the outbreak of the First World War this was hurriedly removed from the counters, only to appear a few weeks later under the more accept-able title of 'Gâteau de Citron'.

But it was the tea itself, the ceremonial of making it, which was the cause of most concern. I wonder what has happened to the charming Victorian silver kettle from which my mother used to warm the cups before I handed them round? This was not only a ceremonial but a pre-caution; the tea-service was very delicate Meissen and cracked all too easily. And the silver-gilt sugar tongs and the Queen Anne sugar bowl . . . I wonder what has happened to them? And the ivory-handled knives for dealing with the scones, should there be any, and the Victorian musical box filled with a sweetmeat that was sold under the name of 'Curiously Strong Peppermints'. These were offered as an aid to digestion and they were certainly very curious; indeed, they nearly blew one's head off.

The scent of peppermints, the tinkle of the music box with its sweet staccato rendering of a theme by Rossini, the white feathers of steam drifting from the boiling kettle, the flicker of flame from the log fire, the ladies' gloves carefully laid on the side-tables, the murmur of conversation, punctuated by the nodding of their hats —wide-brimmed hats with ostrich feathers, tea-cosy hats trimmed with tightly packed Parma violets—the sombre chiming of the grandfather's clock to remind us of the transient nature of all festivities, and then, when the clock struck six, the rustle of silk as the ladies rose from their seats, as though obeying an unheard command, the farewells in the hall, the slamming of carriage doors and, when there was sunshine, the butterfly flutter of parasols, and the clatter of horses' hooves as the last guest swept down the drive.

And my mother at the tea-table, carefully collecting the unconsumed delicacies, which we should have for supper, and the echo of her voice saying 'I think they enjoyed themselves'.

And all of this, remember, because many centuries ago, a random wind directed the leaf of a little shrub towards an emperor's tea-cup.

CHAPTER 14

Cocktail Parties ... Cause and Cure

THE lowest circle of the Inferno is reserved, one hopes, for all those concerned with the invention and the exploitation of the electric guitar. This hideous device has already gone far towards destroying the world, and may eventually destroy it altogether, in the final cacophony that precedes the Day of Judgement. I am among the minority who believe that the Fall of Jericho is to be literally interpreted. The minority, let us never forget, is always right.

In the circle immediately above the guitar fiends, howling their heads off in the depths and bloodying their nails on the tight-stretched strings of their infernal instruments, come the inventors of the cocktail party.

The cocktail party has nothing to recommend itself, physically, economically, or socially. Consider first the physical aspect, which may be most tersely illustrated by an idea which I have long cherished concerning the invitation cards. It should be made compulsory for these cards to conform to the same standards as are enforced upon the tobacco merchants. Thus . . .

The Countess of X
At Home
200 Grosvenor Square, London, W.1
6.30 to 8

ALL INVITATIONS TO COCKTAIL PARTIES
CARRY A GOVERNMENT HEALTH WARNING

For what do cocktail parties do to the body? They demand that the body should be maintained in an erect position for at least an hour, at a period of the day when the body is most urgently in need of relaxation. They also demand that the body's motor, the stomach, should be sharply and swiftly overheated by an injection of fiery fluids with which it was never intended to cope, accompanied by a dust-bin collection of solids in the shape of nuts, olives, cheese straws, and small angry-looking triangles of boot-black caviar. (The average intake of solids at cocktail parties requires at least six hours for digestion.)

What do they do to the mind? If one is a good guest, trying to perform one's duties, they subject the mind to a series of violent pressures of which the most exhausting, in my own case, is a congenital incapacity for remembering people's names. It is not so bad when there are only two of you. One can usually get away with . . . 'Darling . . . such ages since we met . . . and what are you up to *now*?' If one listens very attentively to the answer, which may be quite extensive, one can usually discover, by a process of elimination, what he or she is up to, and whether one is addressing the conductor of the London Symphony Orchestra, an artist, a novelist, a deep-sea-diver, a member of parliament, a film star, an old school chum or . . . if the worst comes to the worst . . . one's hostess. It is when one is joined by a third party that the agony becomes intense, for now one is obliged to

171

perform the introductions. The standard formula, accompanied by a tortured laugh, is . . . 'You know each other, of course . . .' but sometimes this does not work, because it is quite evident that they neither know each other nor wish to do so. Whereupon, one is forced into what I can only call 'Cocktail Esperanto'. A lot of men are called Charles, and one can often get away with a sound like Chlocks, particularly if one has previously filled one's mouth with potato crisps. This token noise, delivered with a bow from the waist, and a graceful wave of the hand towards one's companion, sometimes does the trick. (A word of warning. This technique never works with Americans, who introduce one another as though they were toast masters at a city banquet.)

But perhaps the greatest argument against the cocktail party arises from the time element. If twenty guests arrive at 6.30, another twenty at 7, and the final twenty at 7.30 . . . the first twenty are beginning to go by the time the last twenty arrive, which in itself is enough to cast a gloom over the whole proceedings. Nobody gets a chance to know anybody else, and all the best hors d'œuvres are swiped by the early comers, leaving a group of stragglers frantically munching cheese straws because they have not taken the precaution to arrange for a proper dinner.

So do we give no cocktail parties at all? Yes and no. We can continue to call them 'cocktail parties' if we choose—(the phrase has acquired a convenient mystique) —but we can turn them into something quite different by changing the hour to 7.30, and by making it clear that there will be some sort of hot food. This will eliminate the cheese straws stragglers; it will absolve one from the responsibility of serving a conventional 'dinner'; and it will enable one to play the whole thing by ear. If the party is a flop all the guests will have departed by 10, in a condition of reasonable assuagement. If the party is a success, it may go on till any hour, and there may be one of those magical evenings when somebody sits down at the piano, and there is music, and the flicker of firelight, and the scent of lilies.

Later, I will offer a few recipes—social as well as culinary—for achieving this magic. In the meantime, on a more pedestrian plane, I will suggest that one of the simplest means of achieving it is to begin by serving KEDGEREE, a dish on which some of my own happiest parties have been based.

Somerset Maugham once observed that if we wish to eat well in England we must eat breakfast three times a day. This is no longer the case but there is still a germ of truth in it. The British have a genius for breakfast, and though, on the Continent, they accept the convention of a croissant, a pat of butter, and a minuscule carton of cherry jam, they are always longing, in their heart of hearts, for scrambled eggs, kidneys and bacon, sausages, and of course kedgeree.

Kedgeree has all the party virtues. It is hot, and easy to keep hot. It is cheap—all one needs is smoked haddock, rice, butter, hard-boiled eggs, and flavouring. Most important of all, it could not be easier to negotiate, even if one is standing by an electric fire under a reproduction Van Gogh, elbow-to-elbow with a covey of bores in a howling draught.

Because kedgeree is a standard dish, included in every ABC of Cookery, I will not insult the reader by giving the recipe. But over many years of serving it I have found two ways of brightening it up. The first is to add walnuts, which startle the palate; the second is to tinge the rice with saffron, so that the whole thing seems to have a sunlit glow. As well it should, for saffron comes from crocuses—not the yellow crocuses of spring, as one might expect, but from the dried golden stigmas of the autumn crocuses which, of course, are purple.

Pause for reminiscence.

* * *

Writing of colour takes me back to the parties of the twenties—to Mrs Somerset Maugham in Chelsea, whose parties were always white, and to Elsie de Woolf in Paris, whose parties, as a rule, were predominantly red.

Both these ladies were inclined to carry their passion for their respective signature colours to extremes, particularly in the matter of food. Admittedly, Syrie's white interiors were exquisite . . . white walls, ivory satin curtains, white china vases filled with giant white enamel Chinese camellias, white leather chairs, white sheepskin rugs.

But when these principles were applied to the food, the result was less satisfying, though for sheer audacity Syrie got full marks. Her first white food party is very clear in my memory. On the buffet were towering mounds of white grapes, lit by the glow of tall white candles. There were cold chickens in a white glaze and poached soles with a white sauce. There were white endive salads, and sparkling meringues, and white peppermint creams in white Meissen trays. There were even white crystallized violets—an enchanting conceit which would have enraptured Ronald Firbank. But with all this whiteness, and a curious suspicion that one's inside was being subtly but surely white-washed, one began to long for a bloody steak.

With Elsie de Woolf—Syrie's Franco-American rival —it was the other way round. Everything that could possibly be red was red. Even the lobsters were turned upside down on the crimson table-cloths to emphasize their redness. Flanking the lobsters were joints of very sanguinary beef, carved by decorative young valets in scarlet waistcoats. The salads were of an exceptional redness—beetroot and tomato and red cabbage with a sauce tinted with cochineal. (This sounds disgusting; in fact it was delicious.) And all the wines, needless to say, were red. Even in those distant days they must have been very expensive. Today, they would cost a small fortune.

And yet, as in the case of Syrie, one began to be bored by the redness, and—even as one dipped an out-of-season strawberry into a concoction based on cherry brandy—(equally delicious)—one found oneself longing for a bright yellow banana, which one could take out of the room and peel in the conservatory, accompanied by a young person whose complexion, hopefully, would be firmly pink.

We promised 'magic', and suggested that there were various recipes through which this magic can be achieved. The material recipes can be ignored for the moment, and left to stew in their own juices. There are subtler matters to be considered, for a party, when all is said and done, is a very delicately balanced affair, which, to attain anything like perfection, must be as cunningly orchestrated as a piece of music.

My own small gatherings—which have never hit the headlines—have always been precisely dated. The first week in July, the third week in September, and the fourth week in January. Three parties a year is quite enough to put on the plate of an ageing bachelor.

The reason for these arbitrary date-lines is entirely floral.

The first week in July is the week when the regale lilies are at the peak of their perfection. Though it may sound tiresome, I cannot imagine what life would be like without the perennial enchantment of the lilies, picked from the garden, carried indoors, set in front of mirrors —(after hammering the stalks)—and gloated upon. Sniffed and savoured, preferably in solitude, examined under magnifying glasses, and, of course, set to music. If you are any sort of a pianist, if your fingers retain mobility, and if you find yourself sitting at a Steinway piano in a quiet room, confronted by a keyboard which would hold the answer to all life's problems if one could only master it, the lilies sing to you. They call the tune.

The tunes they have called to me have long since echoed into limbo, but they seemed to be beautiful while they lasted.

So, in July, there is the lily party, which always opens, quite literally, with a gasp, as the guests drift into the music-room and lift up their heads and begin to sniff. It used to be said of Baudelaire that his nose 'ondulait' when he came in contact with exquisite fragrances. The noses of my guests also 'undulate', for wherever they may turn there are lilies, gleaming from every corner, throwing silver shadows from the mirrors.

The September and January parties also have a floral setting. The September one is a red party, with most of the red coming from a dahlia called the Bishop of Llandaff, which is another of those flowers which play a large part in my life. This dahlia has single flowers of a brilliant crimson, which sparkle all the more vividly because the leaves have a coppery sheen. One of my perennial guests is the Bishop of Southwark, who is a party in himself. (The first time he ever called on me he was wearing purple robes, and as soon as he saw the rhododendrons through the window he walked over to them and stood there, looking very magnificent. Then, with great earnestness, he enquired 'Do I match?') The October parties, of course, have no rhododendrons, but they have every other sort of red—great clusters of berries from the firethorn and the mountain ash. The January parties are mainly white, with white hyacinths and narcissi and bowls of snowdrops gathered from a secret wood.

This will be enough about colour for the moment. But before we stroll over to the buffet I should like to mention one way in which a very difficult party—and we have all had to give them—can be saved from complete disaster. If you have reason to believe that all will not be well, there is only one thing to do. Invite one guest, preferably female, who is so socially outrageous that all the other guests, who might else have found that they had little in common, suddenly find themselves united in a psychic bond of communal loathing for the terrible creature.

This was the theme of one of Saki's most delightful stories. He invented a hostess who was obliged to offer weekend hospitality to half-a-dozen people who loathed one another, and in desperation, at the last moment, she invited a seventh guest who was so detestable that people used to leave parties as soon as they saw her enter the room. But on this occasion, marooned in a remote country house, they could not leave, and instead of havoc there was harmony. I was once able to put this precept into practice at a party of my own—by accident rather than design. The party was not going at all well; people were getting stuck in corners, running out of conversation; there were furtive glances at the clock. And then, one of the principal guests—a very famous ballet-dancer —began to get drunk. Nothing could have been more fortuitous. He staggered from group to group, insulting all and sundry, and then precipitated himself into the cloak-room which leads out of the music-room.

After he had emerged, several minutes later, he was followed by Rebecca West—and the name of this great lady is my only excuse for telling the story. For when she returned there was an expression on her face which indicated that she had not been at all amused by the condition in which the young man had left the little cloak-room.

In icy tones she observed . . . 'One would have thought that a ballet-dancer would have had a better . . . *aim.*'

Here is a suggestion for a party dish which seems to be neglected by the average hostess.

Swiss Fondue

This is a dish which might have been specially invented for parties. It is in every way a communal dish, since it is eaten by putting small pieces of bread onto the end of a fork, dipping them into the mixture, devouring them, dipping them again, and going on until one has had enough. Some people of excessive sensitivity seem to think that this is unhygienic, but unless one is in the middle of a small-pox epidemic I can see no objection to it.

Take a shallow earthenware pan, and rub it over with a clove of garlic.

Grate 1 lb of Gruyère cheese with a generous pinch of nutmeg and mix with two wine-glasses of white wine. Any cheap French wine will do, provided that it is not too sweet.

Have ready $\frac{1}{4}$ wine-glass of Kirsch mixed with one teaspoonful of cornflour. (Some experts insist that it must be potato flour, but this is not always available, and cornflour is just as good. Its purpose is not to flavour the fondue but to bind it.)

Have ready 4 egg yolks mixed with $\frac{1}{4}$ pint single cream.

Pour cheese–wine mixture into casserole, and place on gas stove on *an asbestos mat*. This is vital. A fondue that has been allowed to boil is disgusting, and probably lethal.

Turn on gas, watch and pray. Stir with a wooden spoon.

As soon as the cheese–wine mixture is melted, stir in the kirsch–cornflour mixture.

Continue to stir for 2 minutes, and then add the egg–cream mixture.

Bend over the casserole, glare at it, dip a spoon in it, and as soon as it is gooey, snap off the gas, place it on a lighted spirit stove, and carry into the dining-room, hoping that general conversation has not yet begun to flag.

This recipe serves four people, so if you happen to have invited forty, you must multiply the ingredients accordingly.

Its manufacture, as I have described it, sounds as arduous as training for the Olympic games. But it is really quite simple, once you have got the hang of it.

And, I repeat, it is the perfect party dish. It brings people together more quickly than any other dish that has ever been invented. Which, after all, is the object of the exercise.

Curiosa

THIS chapter might come under the heading of 'Believe it or Not'. I have called it 'Curiosa' because it is a hotch potch of various recipes which, when I first learned about them, seemed almost too strange to credit.

One of the strangest is . . .

Silver Chicken

I had to invent this title for the recipe does not appear in any cookery book which I have yet encountered.

You take the largest capon you can buy. It must be a whopper.

You then rinse 6 or 8 silver spoons or forks in hot water. Only silver will do; silver plate would be worse than useless.

Now, taking a firm grip of the chicken, push the silver up its behind. As if this were not enough humiliation, follow it with two heaped tablespoonsful of ground ginger. All this sounds extremely sadistic but it is no more so than keeping the poor thing cramped in a cage for the whole of its unnatural life.

Having maltreated the chicken in this manner, bring a large saucepan of slightly salted water to the boil, put in the chicken, add 6 carrots and 6 medium-size onions, cram on the lid, and boil at the gallop for precisely 5 minutes.

Turn off the gas, lift up the saucepan, transport to the larder, and leave to cool overnight.

On the following morning you must be prepared for a shock. When you lift the chicken out, drain off the water, and remove the spoons and forks, you will find that they have all gone black. Do not be alarmed. A good soaking in any of the modern silver-cleaning preparations will restore them, though this may take rather longer than usual.

A chicken prepared in this manner tastes quite different from any chicken you have ever had before, unless you are at least sixty years old, and can recall the days of your youth, when a chicken really was a chicken, and not a synthetic Robot bird, reared by Robots for the mechanical digestions of other Robots. Apart from the taste, it can be carved in delicate slices, instead of falling to pieces in the manner of the average boiled chicken of today.

Clotted Cream

The only reason for including clotted cream under the heading of 'Curiosa' lies in the fact that so large a number of people appear to imagine that it can only be brought to perfection in the western counties. Hence the legendary titles 'Devonshire Cream' and 'Cornish Cream', and hence the custom of sending tins of the delicacy to one's friends when one is visiting those parts. It is a pleasant convention, and a warmer token of one's esteem than a picture postcard of the Rock Walk at Torquay, but it is really quite unnecessary.

Clotted cream, of the Devonshire or Cornish standard,

can be made as easily in a London suburb as in the lush pastures of the West. There is nothing so special about Cornish cows; they have the same shaped udders and it may be presumed that they think the same thoughts.

And while we are on this subject, here is another curious question. Why have the French—at any rate in Europe—a monopoly of Camembert cheese? What has a French goat got that a British goat hasn't got? Nothing. No larger udders, no deeper thoughts. A goat, as Gertrude Stein never said, is a goat is a goat is a goat. And yet, the average British farmer would blench at the thought of making Camembert.

To revert to our clotted cream.

Perhaps we were wrong to state so unequivocally that anybody can make it, at any time and in any place, because a psychological element does seem to enter into its manufacture. Perhaps there are people with 'cream fingers' just as there are people with 'green fingers'. One thing is certain, you will never make it unless you have a great deal of patience.

It is best to begin by experimenting with comparatively small quantities, which means leaving a note for the milkman telling him to deliver, say, 8 pints on the following morning. You will need to have equipped yourself with a large, wide, shallow earthenware pan. When the milk has arrived and the milkman has recovered from his astonishment, you take the pan to the pantry, and pour in the milk. If the weather is cold it can stay there for up to 24 hours; in summer 12 hours should be enough.

Now comes the heating. In musical terms, this must be largo. If you are cooking on gas, it is essential to turn the gas to its lowest and to place the pan on an asbestos mat.

From now on, it is all a question of waiting, of popping in and out of the kitchen to make sure that the milk is not heating too quickly (even if it begins to boil, ever so slightly, the whole experiment can be written off).

182

It is really a question of cooking with the *eyes*. Watch the surface of the milk, which will slowly begin to undulate. Watch, in particular, the inside rim of the pan, where a solid rim will begin to form. When this rim is thick and golden yellow, the pan may be carried into the larder, provided that your hand is rock steady; otherwise, wheel it on a trolley. It should be left cooling in the larder for at least 12 hours in the summer, and not less than 24 in the winter. Remove with a large spoon or a fish slice.

That is all there is to it, apart from the question of what to do with all the surplus milk. Well . . . most people have neighbours, and stray cats, alas, are always with us.

Postscript. If, on your first attempt, you have any misgivings about the milk failing to clot and being wasted, add a tea cup of single cream. This should ensure success.

Cocktail Curiosity

In Brighton, in the twenties, there lived a sweet old man called Sir Harry Preston who, had he adorned another period, would certainly have been a member of the Prince Regent's set. For though he was not quite a gentleman, and had occasional trouble in pronouncing his h's, he was very rich, extremely sportive, and almost absurdly generous. He was tiny, with a bright mauve complexion, and he had the curious habit of drenching himself every morning in a variety of expensive toilet waters. He applied these so copiously that when he took his promenade along the pier, leaving in his wake a trail of conflicting odours, people would halt in their tracks with an alarmed expression and tiptoe to the railings and stare down into the waters, suspecting that some disaster had befallen a shoal of stranded mackerel.

Failing the Prince Regent, Sir Harry had to content himself with the friendship of the Duke of Windsor who was then, of course, Prince of Wales. They had much to draw them together; they were both very tiny and very rich, they were both extremely fond of sport, especially boxing, and they were both, if one may be forgiven for mentioning it, rather common.

Sir Harry took a fancy to me, which was convenient, because he owned the Royal Albion Hotel, which he said would always be at my disposal. 'Whenever you feel like a breath of hozone, Mr Beverley, give me a ring, and we'll see what Dr Brighton can do for you.' What he did on one occasion was to make me a present of the royal suite, which was full of hozone. The effects were not perhaps so beneficial as might have been anticipated because every morning, at 11.30 precisely, the maître d'hôtel would arrive with a magnum of champagne, followed by the diminutive figure of Sir Harry, who would beckon me to sit with him on the balcony. 'There's nothing like a nice glass of bubbly, Mr Beverley, to set you up for the day.' This may indeed be the case, but when one is presented with a magnum it is socially impossible to confine oneself to a few sips, and one nice glass led to another nice glass and yet another nice glass. The effects of the champagne, the hozone, and the fumes of Sir Harry's toilet waters—which seemed particularly potent at this early hour—did much to undermine the beneficent effects of 'Dr Brighton', and I was obliged to tell him that my capacity for champagne was limited.

After a brief sigh, he brightened. 'Never mind, Mr Beverley, we'll think of something else.'

What he thought of was to appear on the following morning, at precisely the same hour, on a silver tray, and it was far more lethal. It was called . . .

PRESTO POP COCKTAIL

I have the recipe before me, inscribed in his own hand on Royal Albion Hotel writing-paper. (Telegraphic address 'Brilliancy Brighton'.) Though the paper has

shrivelled and yellowed with the passage of more than
half a century it has lost none of its nostalgic appeal.
Here is the recipe.

5 Gallons Booth's Gin.
30 Seville Oranges, using only 1 Peal. [Spelling was not
Sir Harry's strong point.]
30 Lemons, using only 1 Peal.
7½ lbs Granulated Sugar of Sugar Candy or granulated
sugar.
Put into Stone jar to mature for 5 weeks.
Shake frequently.

When I first sipped this concoction Sir Harry informed me that he had created it especially for His Royal
'Ighness, who was 'extremely partial to it'. I can only
assume that he was partial in small quantities; it would
blow most people's heads off. It is really best supped as a
liqueur, from very small glasses, icy cold. To give an
added interest, and to counteract the sweetness, you can
serve it with slices of candied lemon peel.

When one considers the outrageous price of French
liqueurs in these days I think that the Presto Pop is
worthy of a place on the sideboard, though perhaps one
might give it a more appealing name. For myself it will
always have a special appeal by reminding me of a
Brighton that has largely vanished—a Brighton that still
wore some of its former elegance, like a faded shawl, a
Brighton where Prinny life went by to the sound of sea-
gulls and the shade of Prinny still drifted across the
lawns outside the Royal Pavilion.

Flaming Crème de Menthe
This section seems to be verging on the alcoholic, but
since thoughts about food inevitably evoke thoughts
about wine, I make no excuse for bringing this little
curiosity to your attention.

We can best describe it in terms of drama. It is Christmas eve. The guests—six in all—are pleasantly assuaged. The crackers have been pulled; the ash-trays have been emptied and re-emptied. The port has gone round; somebody has lighted a cigar; there is a general sense of well-being. But we are nearing the end of the third act, and a surprise is called for.

The host provides it.

Excusing himself for a moment he exits to the kitchen. He hurries to a dark corner where he has concealed a tray on which he has arranged six liqueur glasses, filled to the brim with crème de menthe. He strikes a match and holds it over the dark green liquid. There is a flicker, another flicker, and then a little flame of peacock blue. He strikes another, and another, until all the glasses are alight. And then, feeling like a mixture between a Walt Disney wizard and one of the minor Borgias, he transports the tray back to the dining-room.

As he opens the door he switches off the lights, so that there is now nothing but candle-light. The guests look up, and gasp—or should gasp, if they have any sensitivity. For the picture of those flickering glasses, in the half-light, is really very pretty indeed. The peacock blue flames are like flowers, like jewels, so beautiful that you forget that you are intended to swallow them.

When you do swallow them, there is yet another surprise. For though the top layer of the crème de menthe is warm, and almost immorally seductive, the bottom layer is icy cold.

A word as to the preparation. Since spirits only produce flames when they are slightly above room temperature, the glasses should be warmed before pouring in the crème de menthe.

A word as to the consumption. After about a minute the rims of the glasses become extremely hot, so that it is wise for each guest to puff out his flame before drinking.

Cuisine for Cats

THE fact that no cookery book, as far as I am aware, has yet devoted any space to the culinary requirements of cats, is a sad comment on our treatment of the feline race.

Day after day women all over the country are busying themselves in their kitchens, bustling to and fro with tempting dishes, stirring pots and pans which emit delicious odours, apparently unaware of the small furry person who is watching them from a safe distance. Indeed, it is all too probable that the cat has been shooed out of the kitchen on the grounds that it is in some curious way 'unhygienic', which is of course total nonsense. A kitchen which is constantly inspected by a conscientious cat is likely to be far more 'hygienic' than a kitchen which does not enjoy the benefit of such supervision.

There are two schools of thought in the art of feline cookery—the Tin School and the Anti-Tin School. Members of the former think almost exclusively in terms of tins, usually because they are too lazy or too unimaginative to do anything else. Members of the latter have a quite unreasonable mistrust of anything that comes out of a tin, either for feline or human consumption. I belong to neither of these Schools—or perhaps it would be more accurate to say that I belong to both.

Let us first consider the Tin School.

I have a rather specialized knowledge of tinned cat foods because some while ago I did a series of television advertisements in praise of one of the most celebrated of these concoctions, called 'Whiskas'. This series was profitable not only to myself but, one hopes, to the cats; it was also very revealing. For quite a number of years I had been in the public eye, in a modest sort of way; there had been the usual number of press photographs which are allotted to popular authors, and the usual number of headlines when one was involved in controversy. Not until the cat advertisements did I attract the sort of public regard which film stars must take for granted. Until then, people had never nudged each other when I sat opposite them in the Tube. For a time I basked in these attentions; here at last was recognition; the laurels of literary achievement were coming my way. But the basking was short-lived. One day, in the Tube, after there had been so much nudging from the opposite seats that I was beginning to 'put on a face' and feel for my fountain pen, a peculiarly repellent female infant, sitting on its mother's knee, thrust at me an accusing finger—(which had been previously embedded in a whipped-cream walnut)—and screamed 'Mummy . . . that's the Whiskas man' which put me squarely in my place.

The interesting thing about the Whiskas episode—if there is anything interesting about it—is the revelation which it gave me of the basic integrity of television advertising, as far, at least, as I have experienced it. For example, on one sweltering morning in July I drove up to the studios to enact a moving scene with a certain Burmese cat whose owner had assured me, and the proprietors (and probably every one else within shouting distance of Wimbledon, where she resided) that her cat, whose name was Buddha, existed solely on Whiskas. This assertion had been checked and rechecked by the office. Buddha, it seemed firmly established, would not deign to consider any other earthly food.

'This,' I thought, as I sweated in the hired Daimler which was transporting me, 'will be an easy one.' I had already approved the stage set, which had a faintly Eastern atmosphere. The lighting was to be dim and mysterious, which might also meet with Buddha's approval. And I had put in an urgent telephone call to stop an earnest underling from banging a gong when Buddha was beginning to sniff the plate. All promised well.

The usual preliminaries went off without a hitch. Between Buddha and myself there was an immediate rapport. He responded most graciously to the techniques of my stroking—which, admittedly, are exceptionally advanced—and marked his approval of my reversed under-the-chin-stroke—(which is of course accompanied by a gentle pulling of the tail)—by breaking into a loud purr.

'I think we can take the first shot now,' said the director. 'Lights!'

The lights blazed up, everybody scurried to his position, and the make-up girl darted out to bang me on the nose with a powder puff.

'Silence, everybody, please! If you'd take your place, Mr Nichols? Yes, kneeling on the rug, as we decided. Thank you. May we have the Whiskas, please? Thank you. You can take Buddha now, and if you can keep him purring it'd be marvellous.'

In a deathly hush, Buddha was handed to me, still purring. 'Don't forget to smile when you say the opening line,' murmured the director. 'O.K. Get rolling.' The clapper-boy gave the usual signal, the cameras began to roll. We had begun.

I looked straight into the camera, smiling like mad, and in dulcet tones announced to the world . . . 'The name of this beautiful creature is . . . (dramatic pause) . . . Buddha! And what do you think he has for breakfast?' (Transfer smile to Buddha, place him on floor, wave right hand towards plate.) 'Whiskas!'

Whereupon Buddha, having given one sniff of the Whiskas, shudders with repulsion, turns a pale pink bottom dead on to the camera, and stalks off into the wings, where he is clasped into the arms of his owner, the Wimbledon woman.

'Cut', cries the director. 'Douse lights.'

He does not seem greatly perturbed. After all, this sort of thing has happened before; it always does, in animal pictures. I get off the floor, closely pursued by the make-up girl, who continues to bang me on the nose with the powder puff. I join the director, who is questioning the Wimbledon woman.

'Is he usually as temperamental as this?' he enquires politely.

'He is *never* temperamental,' she retorted. 'Does he *look* temperamental?'

Personally I thought he looked exceedingly temperamental, especially when viewed from the rear, but it might not be wise to say this. So I asked if she was sure that he hadn't had his breakfast already? At which she bridled. Of course she was sure. In tragic tones she proclaimed, 'Not a bite has he had, the poor lamb!'

From the expression on the poor lamb's face, he did not seem to be unduly distressed by this deprivation. He wore a broad smirk and was obviously enjoying himself. All cats like being the centre of attention.

Director. 'Well, let's have another go.'

So we had another go. And another, and another. Always with the same result. 'Lights! O.K. Get rolling!' Clappers. Smile. Dulcet accents. 'The name of this beautiful little creature is . . . (dramatic pause) . . . Buddha! And what do you think he has for breakfast? Whiskas!'

After about the eleventh attempt I began to suspect that Buddha had breakfasted off a substantial portion of cold grouse, for his reaction was quite invariable. A glance at the Whiskas, a shudder of distaste, and a swift expert switch of his pale pink bottom, dead on, to the camera, followed by an exit to the wings. If there had been the faintest suspicion that he was alarmed by the lights or distressed by the noise, I should have called the whole thing off, lifted him into his basket, and sent him home to Wimbledon with a purr. But he was not in the least alarmed. He was having a ball.

Standing there, stroking this wicked, adorable creature, I turned to the director and made an immoral suggestion. 'Don't you think we could cheat it?'

'How do you mean, cheat it?' There was a chill in his voice.

'Well . . . couldn't somebody go out into the Edgware Road and get a fillet of sole?'

Silence from the director and from the Wimbledon woman.

I refused to be abashed. 'And then we could bury the fillet of sole in the Whiskas, and Buddha would gobble it up and nobody would be any the wiser.'

The hostile reaction to this very sensible suggestion was so immediate and so evidently genuine that the reader may now understand what I meant when I referred to 'The essential integrity of television advertising'. The Wimbledon woman looked as though I were intent upon indecent assault. So did the director. Obviously, he observed, in iceberg accents, I was joking. Obviously I was unaware of the ethics of the advertising community. (Too true.) Obviously I had never heard of Clause Something or Other in the Trades Something or Other Act which laid down that if advertisers were found guilty of fraud or deceit in the commercial presentation of something or other, the people perpetrating the fraud would involve themselves in penalties worse than death. All this was true. I had heard of none of these things.

So we called it a day. And that is why the great British public never discovered, and never will, what Buddha has for breakfast.

Tail piece. The studio has emptied. The lights are dimmed. The electricians have departed and, thank God, so has the make-up girl, because my nose has taken about as much Max Factor as it can absorb. And I am left alone with the Wimbledon woman, who is preparing to put Buddha into his basket.

But where has he gone? There is a moment's panic and then, in the distance, I recognize a familiar pink behind. It belongs of course to Buddha. And what is he doing? He is avidly devouring the large plateful of Whiskas which he has been so scornfully spurning for the past three hours.

Which goes to show that some cats, like some humans, prefer to breakfast in private.

I have not told this story in order to give a boost to a particular cat food—(though it happens to be the sort that my own cats prefer)—but to help to dispel the mistrust which some people still have about tinned cat foods in general. Even so, I think that cats are entitled to a variety of choice, and my own shelves are loaded with a very wide selection. Some of these are instantly and haughtily rejected; others are gobbled up for a few days and then, quite unaccountably, despised. Why not? We have these mysterious tastes and aversions ourselves. Why should we deny them to our cats?

Now for the Anti-Tin point of view.

One of the strongest arguments in favour of this school of thought is contained in the fact that all cats, when given the opportunity, go out into the garden to have an occasional nibble of grass. Very pretty they look while doing so, sitting in the shadow of the copper beech, where they seem to have decided that the grass grows sweetest. Presumably they need the 'roughage' which the grass must give them.

If you have no garden, I think that you should contrive that they have this roughage in some other form. At first this may sound impractical; no cat, obviously, would look twice at a salad that had been covered with French dressing. But if you persevere you will be surprised by the approval with which your efforts are greeted. For instance, my own tabby cat 'Leo' has a passion for raw cucumber. I first discovered this on a hot summer afternoon when I had been preparing a cucumber salad. Most of it had been sliced and salted and carried into the larder to cool, but I had left the unpeeled butt end on the kitchen table. When I returned Leo was on the table, gnawing it with evident ecstasy, and when I put out my hand to rescue it, he thrust out his paw to guard it, glared at me, and growled. This, of course, was the highest form of compliment; if a cat growls when you attempt to take his food away it means that the dish is being fully appreciated. I have often thought how pleasing it would be if one's dinner guests could adopt this charming uninhibited procedure and if —when one was preparing to clear the table for the next course—they thrust their hands over their plates, and growled. Although it might interrupt the conversation, it would be highly flattering for the cook.

Cats show remarkable ingenuity in their efforts to obtain this essential vitamin, or whatever it should be called, in their diet. I once had an adorable black kitten who suddenly developed the complaint which used to be called bad breath but must now, in this genteel era, be described as 'halitosis'. When it scampered in from the garden, one summer morning, sprang onto my knee, and breathed this disturbing odour into my face, I was not only dismayed but bewildered. I felt like saying 'This is out of character; you are behaving, not like a cat, but like a human being. If you were human, one would not be at all surprised that you should smell unpleasant; indeed, one would be surprised if you did not. And one would give you every encouragement to gargle, and chew lozenges, and anoint yourself with sprays and ointments, because humans who omit these precautions—especially when gathered together in considerable assemblies—are admittedly insupportable. But cats—no. Cats have, or should have, a fragrance of cleanly washed fur, warm paws scented with mud, and moss and autumn leaves and the bark of freshly scratched tree trunks.'

It was all rather disturbing, and I decided that if the disorder persisted I would have to send for the Vet. Then, later in the day, the mystery was solved. I had gone out into the garden to call the kitten in for his tea, and was worried when he did not answer the tapping of the plate, which serves the purpose of a gong. He was not sitting by the pond, supervising the goldfish, nor sleeping under the copper beech, nor perched in any of the trees. Tapping more and more urgently, I made my way to the herb garden, and there I found him, and understood. He was sitting in the middle of a clump of chives, biting large bunches of them and chewing them with the greatest relish. When I lifted him up he breathed fumes of astonishing potency; no human being could have emitted an odour more alarming. However, I could not reproach him; he was safe and sound, and he had taught me a lesson. All the same, I put a cloche over the chives—or what was left of them—and directed his attention to a bed of parsley, which he seemed to like just as well.

The moral of all this is that we should use a little imagination, and realize that if cats like strange foods, they probably have good reasons for liking them.

I only wish that we could return to the days of Doctor Johnson, whose cat—by name Hodge—was constantly regaled on a diet of oysters.

Postscript on Milk

There is a legend, widely held by persons whose feline adjustments are immature, that if they give a cat a saucer of milk they have done their duty to it for the rest of the day. This is a total fallacy and, I suspect, another sign of human laziness. Much sentimental nonsense has been written about giving pussy cats saucers of milk, and countless Victorian oleographs have been designed in celebration of this subject. What could be sweeter than a picture of a dainty female infant pouring a pale yellow stream into a pale blue cup while a Persian kitten— throttled by a pale pink ribbon—gazes at her with adoring eyes?

If I had ever found a female infant bending over a saucer of milk in such a posture I should have been sorely tempted—after removing the pale pink ribbon— to rub her nose in it. Not only is milk an inadequate diet for a cat, but many cats actively dislike it. I once had a cat called 'Five' whose loathing for milk was so strong that he could not even look at it. When he saw the others drinking it he stalked past them, averting his eyes and went over to his bowl of water, which he lapped very loudly and with a very superior expression, like a vege-tarian showing off in a steak house. Provided that a cat has a full diet in other respects, milk is probably less essential than water. At any rate, 'Five' seemed to thrive on it. He died in my arms, one Christmas eve, at the age of twenty-one, and the last thing that touched his lips, before he drifted away to hunt in the Elysian fields, was a wad of cotton wool, soaked in water from the tap.

Mayonnaise

I SOMETIMES think that mayonnaise has an almost mystic significance. From the way in which it is composed and the extent to which it is appreciated you can read the character, not only of individuals but of nations. Although the *Oxford Dictionary* dates its invention from the year 1841, this is an arbitrary allocation that we need not take too seriously, for it is impossible to imagine the history of France at any period without the civilizing influence of this simple but inspired concoction, which must surely have sparkled in silver dishes on the banqueting tables of le Roi Soleil. It goes with the flesh tints of Boucher and belongs among the picnics of Fragonard. And for many of us, in the days when we still travelled to Europe by sea instead of by air it was the real beginning of our holiday, the first authentic evidence that we were truly 'abroad'. As soon as we took our seats in the restaurant car of the Golden Arrow at Calais, and tasted the œufs à la Russe which were always included in the hors d'œuvres, we realized that we had returned to civilization and that for the moment, at least, we were safe from the gastronomic assaults of the barbarians, as typified in bottled 'salad cream'.

If we were to say what we really felt about bottled mayonnaise and the people who sell it, naming names, we should be involved in several million pounds' worth of libel actions, because in America—(whence the horror originated)—and in the rest of the English-speaking world, the manufacture of bottled mayonnaise is a giant industry. So let us content ourselves by suggesting that it is one of the major sources of cultural pollution, and that the self-respecting cook should transfer it to the medicine chest, where its only purpose would be to serve it as an instant emetic.

In the contemporary kitchen the use of bottled mayonnaise—or 'salad cream' as it is sometimes called—is even less excusable than in the past, because with the invention of the Electric Mixer it is now as easy to make as a cup of tea. And yet, even to this day there are still reputable cooks who continue to insist that it should be prepared by hand. One of the most widely read authorities in the British press recently devoted no less than three columns to the subject, treating it as though she were describing an intricate surgical operation, waxing almost hysterical about the dangers which lay in wait for the unskilful— how an extra spoonful of vinegar might cause the whole concoction to curdle—how a faulty flick of the wrist might bring disaster—how the mayonnaise could be 'rescued' at the last moment by the addition of an extra egg or another pinch of dry mustard, etc., etc.

All this is nonsense. There is only one justification for making mayonnaise by hand—a psychological one. It is a process which is extremely good for the nerves. In the old Ante-Mixer days, when my temper was on edge and when life seemed more than usually difficult, I sometimes went out to the kitchen and made a mayonnaise as a means of letting off steam. The tenser the mood, the more

197

acute the irritation, the better the mayonnaise; there seemed to be an extra power to one's elbow, and an inspired abandon in one's manipulation of the oil. There was never a sign of curdling, and when it was all over one felt strangely relaxed.

However, this therapy might not be effective with everyone; indeed, like all psychological treatment it might go into reverse. As in the case of a friend of mine who was recovering from a nervous breakdown. She had been advised by her specialist to devote several hours a day to the contemplation of tropical fish. Their gentle movements as they glided through their green, shadowy pleasaunces would . . . so he assured her . . . put her at peace with the world. They did nothing of the sort. They bored her so acutely that one night she broke down again, emptied the poor creatures into a large saucepan and was only just prevented, at the last moment, from turning them into fish soup. As I am among those who believe that fishes have feelings I am glad to be able to record that neither the fishes nor the lady were the worse for their misadventure. Here is our recipe for . . .

INSTANT MAYONNAISE (Half pint)

Ingredients	Timing
Seize two eggs. Crack them, whites and all, and hurtle them into mixer.*	5 seconds
Grasp bottle of wine vinegar and shoot in two tablespoonsful.	4 seconds
Dash in a $\frac{1}{2}$ teaspoonful of salt and flick in a $\frac{1}{2}$ teaspoonful dry mustard.	5 seconds
Take a deep breath, glance at second-hand of your watch, and switch on lever of mixer. As you do so pour in half a pint of oil, in a steady stream. If you must use olive oil, do so, but corn oil is almost as good, and very much cheaper.	3 seconds

There now ensues a period of 60 seconds of uproar, at the end of which, when you switch the lever off, you will be confronted with a smooth, pearly, exquisitely flavoured concoction which you could set before a Queen.

All in the space of 1 minute and 17 seconds.

I make no apologies for the breathless prose in which the recipe is presented; it was necessary to write in this style in order to stress the fact that the making of perfect mayonnaise is 'as easy as making a cup of tea'.

*Comments

'Whites and all.' The suggestion that we should use the whites as well as the yolks may cause a certain amount of eyebrow-raising in circles of haute cuisine. In the 'classic' mayonnaise, you use only the yolks and what you do with the whites is your own affair. (You can make meringues out of them, if you know how to make meringues.) What usually happens, in my own experience, is that you conscientiously pour the whites into a tumbler which you place in the refrigerator, where it remains for several weeks until one day you discover that it is covered with a sinister green mould. Whereupon you throw it down the sink.

So it is really simpler, and certainly more economical, to use the whites. Fanatical Mixer Fans maintain that you can actually put in the shells as well, claiming that these will disintegrate in the flash of an eye, and that they are full of calcium which is 'good for making bones'. I do not subscribe to this school of thought. I have enough bones already and I have no desire, at my time of life, to have any more.

Tail Piece

THIS seems as good a place as any for closing the
kitchen door, and there may be many to tell me
that I should never have dared to open it. But as
we have seen, I was obliged to open it, and when I did I
found it was a chamber of mysteries and a treasure-trove
of memories. To solve the mysteries was a challenge; to
recall the memories was a consolation.

That is what cooking has come to mean to me. A
challenge and a consolation. Among the drawbacks of
growing old is the increasing recurrence of the feeling
of déja vu. One has crossed the five continents and swum
the seven seas; one has heard most of the great music,
seen most of the great pictures, read most of the great
books; and though one often returns to these for refreshment, their power to inspire is dimmed by repetition.
Only too often, the elderly meet this situation by sighing
and sinking into arm-chairs and switching on the television, which is in itself a form of living death. They

would do better to walk out in a howling gale, sit down on a patch of damp moss, and swiftly expire with dignity and resignation.

But they would do better still by walking into the kitchen and learning what it has to teach them. Here is a domain where at least they will not be constantly reminded of the decay of their physical function. One does not have to do acrobatics on the gas stove; a great many things can be prepared sitting down. Nor will they be humiliated by the improvement of other elementary assets, such as the sense of smell. In the elderly this is as sharp as it was when they were in their teens, and it is among life's subtle pleasures, on which the kitchen plays endless variations . . . the sweet scent of mint, the curious aroma of cloves, the fresh fragrance of fennel, the animal tang of ginger, the cool feminine perfume of nutmeg, the hot masculine challenge of garlic.

And always, of course, there will be the new stimuli sustained by their own palates. Some of these, no doubt, will be extremely unpleasant, at the outset of their careers, but they will not be lethal. And when they achieve success their happiness, particularly if it can be shared by their contemporaries, is in itself a form of rejuvenation.

The pleasures of the table are among the last to leave us in the long banquet of life. I hope to enjoy them for a few more years to come.